# Who Should Read This Book

This book is not just for Jewish people. It is for anyone who is open to recovery-oriented teachings that can be gleaned from the Bible and the teachings of Jewish tradition.

✔ People who want to enrich their understanding of the Twelve Steps with Bible-based teachings

✔ Everyone facing the struggles of daily living who looks for insight and guidance from the Bible as a source of faith, strength, hope, and spiritual wisdom

✔ People in Twelve Step recovery programs

✔ Alcoholics and addicts, compulsive gamblers, those with eating disorders and sexaholics—and those who care about them

✔ Individuals who seek an authentic spiritual foundation for spiritual living based in sacred texts

✔ Rabbis, priests, and ministers—clergy who want to counsel congregants and parishioners spiritually

✔ Psychiatrists, psychologists, therapists providing religious meaning in the counseling context

✔ Codependents who live in or grew up in a dysfunctional family

✔ Jews and non-Jews from all walks of life

✔ Jews whose spiritual awakening might lead them to take a fresh, adult look at the religion of their birth

✔ All people who read *Twelve Jewish Steps to Recovery: A Personal Guide for Turning from Alcoholism and Other Addictions* (Jewish Lights Publishing, 1991)

# Renewed Each Day

**Daily Twelve Step
Recovery Meditations
Based on the Bible**

*Volume* I
**Genesis & Exodus**

*Rabbi Kerry M. Olitzky
&
Aaron Z.*

Foreword by **Rabbi Michael A. Signer**
Afterword by **JACS Foundation**

*Renewed Each Day: Daily Twelve Step Recovery Meditations Based On the Bible, Volume I: Genesis and Exodus*

For information regarding permission to reprint material from this book, please mail or fax your request in writing to Jewish Lights Publishing, Permissions Department, at the address / fax number listed below, or e-mail your request to permissions@jewishlights.com.

© 1992 by Kerry M. Olitzky and Aaron Z.

**Library of Congress Cataloging-in-Publication Data**
Olitzky, Kerry M., 1954–
   Renewed each day: daily twelve step recovery meditations based on the Bible, v. 1: Genesis & Exodus / Kerry M. Olitzky & Aaron Z.

Includes bibliographical references (p. 176)
   1. Twelve-step programs—Religious aspects—Judaism—Meditations. 2. Bible. O.T. Pentateuch—Meditations. 3. Compulsive behavior—Religious aspects—Judaism. 4. Substance abuse—Religious aspects—Judaism. I. Z., Aaron, 1954– II. Title.
BM538.T85045   1992
296.7'2—dc20                                                            92-8517
                                                                                  CIP

ISBN-13: 978-1-879045-12-5 (quality pbk.)
ISBN-10: 1-879045-12-5 (quality pbk.)

First edition
ISBN: 978-1-68336-262-3 (hc)

Manufactured in the United States of America

Illustrations by Maty Grünberg
Cover design by Nancy Malerba

Published by Jewish Lights Publishing
www.jewishlights.com

For Toby Geller, M.D., Joseph Zullo, M.D., and Lewis Amoroso, M.D., healers of body and soul through whose hands God has renewed the miracle of life.

KERRY M. OLITZKY

To my wise-hearted wife, Elaine, you angel you . . .

AARON Z.

# Contents

## Volume I

### Genesis

### Exodus

# Volume II

# Acknowledgments

If you believe as we do in the Yiddish notion of *bashert* (things just happen), then the bringing together of two people to prepare these volumes happened according to a plan whose comprehension is beyond us. Certain things are just meant to be. Hence, two authors from different walks of life came together to teach Torah and recovery because of a mutual interest in helping people in recovery on their spiritual journey. But no book is the sole work of any two individuals. There are many people whose words are spoken through our voices and who deserve our recognition and thanks.

To colleagues and friends at Hebrew Union College-Jewish Institute of Religion who constantly offer support and encouragement, I express my abiding gratitude. In particular, I mention Rabbi Alfred Gottschalk, president; Rabbi Paul Steinberg, vice president and dean of faculty; and Rabbi Norman Cohen, dean. These men are truly teachers of Torah and provide me with Torah wisdom each day.

While words are inadequate, I also thank my family. In my wife, Sheryl, God truly created for me a sheltering angel who is my life. The young, innocent interest and pride expressed by our children, Avi and Jesse Olitzky, buoy my efforts and instill my words and acts with ultimate meaning.

RABBI KERRY M. OLITZKY
*Hebrew Union College—*
*Jewish Institute of Religion, NY*

To Rabbi Jeff, for keeping Torah "green" for me; my sponsor, Bob, for his warmth, wisdom, and healing laughter; friends and supporters of the "Nyecker Rebbe"; JACS buddies Fran, Larry, Ephraim, and Shlomo; old friends Jeff, Austin, and Alan W., who were there in the beginning; fellowship friends Paul, Alan, Steve O., Mike M., and all those I haven't yet met—it does work; my brother Jed, a co-survivor; my children, Yosef, Eliahu, and Milke Rivke Yehudit, three blessings beyond my wildest dreams; and, last and first, the Holy Presence, for miracles and blessings both known and hidden, the gifts of Torah and recovery, and for renewing creation this day.

AARON Z.

## Acknowledgments

All of the folks at Jewish Lights truly help fill the world with light. Publishers Stuart and Antoinette Matlins make the creation of a book a holy task. Likewise do Jevin Eagle and Carol Gersten provide direction and purpose to our work. And to our editor, Sara Brzowsky, whose insightful pen illuminated our every word, we offer thanks.

We also want to express our appreciation to those who shared their thoughts and joined them with our own: Rabbis Neil Gillman, Lawrence Hoffman, and Harold Schulweis, Danny Siegel and Dr. Ben Zion Twerski. And to those individuals and organizations who graciously allowed us to include their prayers and insights, we give voice to an abiding gratitude: Rabbi Lionel Blue and the Reform Synagogues of Great Britain, Rabbi Sidney Greenberg and Prayer Book Press, Rabbi Jules Harlow and the Rabbinical Assembly, Rabbi Zalman Schacter-Shalomi and the P'nai Or Fellowship, and Joseph Yordan and the JACS Foundation.

KERRY M. OLITZKY & AARON Z.

# Foreword

## The Spiritual Journey
## to Recovery through Torah

The spiritual journey which leads to recovery often begins outside the Judaism of our family origin. For many people, the study of Torah or any document of the Jewish tradition is linked to painful memories of childhood. We were forced to attend Hebrew School, Religious School, or weekly Sabbath worship. Knowledge of Judaism was associated with a parent or grandparent whose presence in our lives evokes painful feelings. There are those who come to the rooms of Twelve Step programs feeling that their surrender to the spiritual path would be a disappointment to the Jewish community. For these people, Torah study is a reminder that they were "not enough." Judaism and its sacred texts become a constant reminder of how far they have fallen. They maintain that recovery in a Twelve Step program is enough for them. From their perspective, the spirituality of their group is sufficient without the additional demands of Torah study

If the path to recovery means that "we will not regret the past nor wish to shut the door on it," then the readings in this book can lead us back beyond the painful memories. By studying and meditating on verses of the Torah and Jewish tradition one day at a time, we may be able to change our perspective. If Torah represented a dark, unhappy memory in the past, then perhaps through the perspective of our recovery it now can shed great light and bring us to peace of mind and serenity. Torah can bring us healing.

As we read each week's Torah portion and corresponding meditation, we can come to believe that it brings God's love to us. Our prayerbook tells us:

> With a great love You have loved us Adonai, and You have shown us overwhelming tenderness. For the sake of Your great name and for the sake of our ancestors who trusted in You, You have taught us the laws of life. Have mercy upon us, and teach us. Put into our hearts the ability to understand, obey, learn, teach, observe, and perform all the words of Your teachings.

Ultimately, the study of Torah is a reciprocal relationship of love between us and God. The prayerbook understands that God gave us words of Torah not in order to judge our adherence to them, but out of love for us. We in turn learn Torah not to be judged, but to demonstrate love for God through our actions.

Our study of Torah on a weekly basis is not like our study of biology or law. It is not about how "smart" we are or how brilliant our comment on the portion studied may appear to a friend or neighbor. *Talmud Torah,* the study of Torah, is not simply reading; it is a meditative process of looking at ourselves in the mirror. This mirror enables us to see ourselves from the perspective of our tradition and its search for God. We will be able to read and relate to stories that at earlier periods of our lives we simply dismissed as fables.

Reading for holiness, *Talmud Torah,* permits us to approach our texts with a different frame of reference. When we read something that is in conflict with our way of understanding the world, we will not ask if it is true or false. Rather, we will ask, "What does it mean? How can I apply it to my life?" If something in Torah seems to contradict our "modern" view of the world, we can now ask, "Why am I so bothered by this passage?" The truth of Torah becomes the way in which it helps us grow toward a deeper peace of mind. Torah study is then part of our Eleventh Step work, where we seek through prayer and meditation to improve our conscious contact with God as we understand God. As we do our "searching and fearless moral inventory," Torah reading gives us another way to search deep into our hearts and souls.

Each weekly portion provides another step toward reuniting with the story of how our Jewish community through the generations made this same search for God. It requires us, even as it required them, to be really present to God. As we read Torah, we observe how often the response to God's word is *Hineini,* "I am present." What we often miss is how often God appears in the Torah as a presence. When announcing the Divine name to Moses, God's choice is *Ehiyeh,* "I am present to you." Rabbis in later generations understood this four-letter name, YHWH, to represent God's attribute of mercy. Thus, most of the commandments and speeches delivered in the Torah derive from God's love and mercy. As the Israelites wander in the desert, they build a Sanctuary in their midst, and they feel God's presence manifest through a cloud or pillar of smoke. Words and images in Torah remind us of the importance of a higher spiritual presence in our lives.

Most of us know the names of the five books of Torah from the Greek translation: Genesis, Exodus, Leviticus, Numbers, and Deuteronomy. However, each of them has a Hebrew name, and these Hebrew names reveal a significant perspective on the message of Torah in our recovery. In a sense, each Hebrew name indicates a part of the journey toward the Promised Land. This journey from chaos to the Promised Land parallels the passage those in recovery make from the darkness of their despair toward serenity.

The first book of Torah is called *Bereishit,* or "beginnings" in Hebrew. It reveals all the problems of beginnings, starting with the utter chaos before the cosmos. The beginnings of the Torah journey are in setting boundaries or limits. Light is divided from darkness. Noah is divided from a morally corrupt universe. Even God sets limits on the Divine power after the destruction of creation. Then the search for the Divine begins in earnest with Abraham and Sarah, Isaac and Rebecca, and Jacob, Leah, and Rachel. In each set of narratives, they discover meaning in their lives by acknowledging God. Reciprocally, God nurtures and cares for them. What binds these stories together is the concept of *brit* or covenant. Faith and trust are demanded of both parties, human and Divine. None of the characters in *Bereishit* are perfect. There are many conflicts between the peoples, parents, and children, who make progress yet never achieve perfection. By the conclusion of the book, we have moved beyond the boundaries of the Promised Land into Egypt.

The second book of Torah is called *Shemot,* or "names." Once we move from the setting of limits and boundaries in a nurturing relationship, we can call things by their proper name. In this book, the Israelites as a community learn the same lesson which their ancestors learned as individuals. God cares for them and will nurture them but will not tolerate chaos. At the beginning of this book, we learn the name of the teacher who guides and leads them on their journey, Moses. Before he can lead others, Moses experiences humiliation, pain, and alienation. Yet, from the presence of God, Moses draws sufficient strength to accomplish more than he ever thought he could. In *Shemot,* we learn how the Israelites are delivered from the pain of slavery and make their own covenant—as a collective body—at Sinai. God's response is to deliver a set of principles and laws by which they can live. No sooner do they agree to live by the principles grounded in acknowledging God, than the Israelites slip back into the chaos of idolatry with the Golden Calf. Moses remains steadfast, and God renews the covenant of nurturing and caring. By the end of this book, a Sanctuary for God's presence is established by the people who previously had preferred Egyptian slavery or a Golden Calf.

The third book of Torah is *Vayikra,* "and God called." It describes the difficult process by which the Israelites learned how they could maintain their contact with God on a daily basis. This biblical book is one that often seems alien to our modern sensitivities. What can we learn about recovery from long passages that focus on how the blood of animals was splashed against an altar in the desert? The Hebrew title provides us with an important clue. How *does* God call *us?* What draws us near to God? How do we assemble in community to acknowledge God's presence? The answer to these questions would seem to be, *in the details.* Once we acknowledge the need for recovery and gain some knowledge of who and what we are, we need a form to maintain our relationship with our Higher Power, as well as with other human beings. *Vayikra* provides us with models for what constitutes misdeeds or sins, how human beings can reconcile their grievances with one another and with God. The final chapters of the book remind us that all money, property, and prestige are part of a spiritual relationship with God.

In the fourth book of Torah, *Bemidbar,* "in the Desert," we observe the period of wandering and the struggle to maintain holiness. It is clear that this is a story of progress and not perfection. Moses and the community frequently disagree. They fight over power and authority. When the chance to reach the Promised Land is put forward, many want to shrink back from the challenge. The first encounters with people who are not part of the Israelite covenant appear in this book. This results in a blessing from a non-Israelite prophet. Reading *Bemidbar* from the perspective of recovery can teach us that our day-by-day journey, "slips" and all, leads to blessing.

The fifth book of Torah, *Devarim,* or "words," provides some real surprises. From the end of *Bemidbar,* we might have assumed that the journey into the Promised Land was only a few battles away. Instead, we learn that the Promised Land is never conquered within the literary boundaries of Torah. Instead of ultimate achievement, we have a majestic series of speeches which review the voyage of God and the Israelites. The theme of a nurturing covenant, where both human beings and God set limits and obey them is central to *Devarim*. Faithfulness is the key to the "blessings" and the "curses" which are offered to the Israelites. What they take with them into the Promised Land are the "words" which they live by. Above all, they are urged to "choose life in order that you might live." If they ever feel inadequate to the obligations of the covenant, they are reminded, "The commandment which I give you is not in the heavens that you should ask who will go up into the heavens and bring it to us . . . but it is very near to you, in your mouth and in your heart that you might do it." Another important aspect of the final book of Torah is that the great teacher Moses dies before reaching the Promised Land. No one knew the location of his grave. By this, the Israelites learned to place principles before personalities.

"Beginnings," "Names," "And God Called," "In the Desert," and "Words": These are the paths that Torah sets before us. We can make them *our* story. We must emerge from our beginnings; learn the characteristics that constitute us; gain a sense of our own vocation; and live with the meaning of that vocation. Only then do we have the right words to pass on to others.

It is not a road of perfection but a road to perfection. From the words of Torah in this book and the traditional commentaries that are part of the daily meditations, we get a sense of the healing power that Torah has to offer. If we are willing to meditate on Torah it can be for each of us—

> A Tree of Life for them that hold fast to her, and whoever holds on to her is happy. Her ways are ways of pleasantness and all her paths are peace.

To these words from the book of Proverbs, our prayerbook adds a line from the book of Lamentations: "Take us back, O Adonai, to Yourself, and let us come back. Renew our days as of old." What better expression of Twelve Step recovery could we find?

RABBI MICHAEL A. SIGNER

# *Introduction*

My name is Aaron, and I'm a Jewish addict.

I am also married, a father of three children, a New York-area homeowner, over-educated, self-employed, frequently funny, thirtysomething, from the Bronx, a longtime Mets, Bob Dylan, and Grateful Dead fan, a voracious reader, and a whole lot of other semi-interesting stuff. But, for the purpose of this book, the main thing you need to know about me is that I'm a Jewish addict.

As a Jew, I am affiliated with an egalitarian Conservative synagogue in the New York metropolitan area. I had a Modern Orthodox upbringing, but my parents could not afford to send me to yeshiva. I did attend Yeshiva University's "beginner program" for two years but then transferred to a city college as drugs, sex, and rock 'n' roll seduced me away from the initial—and genuine—spiritual awakening that had led me to Yeshiva. I consider myself a Sabbath observer and keep a kosher home. I attend Shabbat services regularly but late. I am active in my synagogue's Men's Club, particularly with regard to Sunday morning softball and the yearly Super Bowl deli-laden bash. I don't wear *tzitzit* or a yarmulke, but my youngest son does. My two school-age children both attend a very *heimishe* Modern Orthodox day school. We celebrate all the Jewish holidays, read the Jewish newspapers, support Jewish causes, attend Jewish-topic lectures of interest, and have an extensive Jewish home library, as my wife and I are major book-lovers.

All this is to say that, as a Jew, I consider myself to be fairly normal. If anything, I am probably more knowledgeable and more observant than most in the American Jewish community.

And I am just as firmly and unmistakably an addict. I can more easily tell you how I became Jewish than why I became an addict—I was born Jewish. I don't quite know why I became an addict. Oh sure, I could spend a few pages reviewing childhood shame and self-esteem issues. I could talk about the sixties and how drugs were more socially and even spiritually acceptable then, but the fact is that a lot of people weaned themselves off drugs, and I kept right on going. I could even talk about how ours is a "quick-fix" culture and how many forces in our society conspire to make us feel "less than," but the fact is that we are all exposed, to some degree, to those forces—and only some of us choose a chemical solution.

So I can not adequately explain why I became an addict. I can, however, tell you *how* I became one: I used drugs until drugs used me. Until it hurt. And long afterward.

I used despite my religious upbringing, despite thousands of dollars of psychiatric therapy, and despite the care and concern of those around me. I was bright, but I kept on using. I was socially acceptable, but that just played into my denial. I kept quitting, but I couldn't stay quit. I tried so hard, so desperately hard, to recreate the "good old days," when drugs were, for me, such innocent, carefree fun—an exercise in futility that lapsed over into a kind of insanity that put me irrevocably over the line.

I started with pot in 1971, when I was seventeen, and it made me feel more comfortable with myself than anything in my life had up until that point. Along the way, I tried LSD (about a dozen times), mescaline, quaaludes, hashish, valium, and, to a much lesser degree, "ups" (speed) and "downs" (barbiturates). I never became much of a drinker, but I do recall getting drunk enough at parties to become sick and/or really hung over about once or twice a year during my late teens and early twenties.

Drugs were downright desirable then, even necessary. They were considered a potent tool for spiritual growth, social change, radical self-transcendence, and off-the-planet sex. They cemented social relationships, helped establish new ones more "spontaneously," and helped define my generation. At the time, I believed these things. I felt there was a profoundly spiritual aspect to getting high. You became more open to the idea of alternate realities and the interconnectedness of all things. Society was far too joyless and straitlaced—it *needed* some serious loosening up. Besides, how could anyone ever figure out what the lyrics to a Bob Dylan or Grateful Dead song meant *unless* they were high?

The important thing was to use drugs "responsibly," and, for a long time (about ten years), I was quite adept at maintaining some semblance of control. I kept up my grades. I got married, stayed steadily employed, and even started my own successful business. I was very "socially acceptable"—a weekend, intersession, and summer-vacation user. And then the weekends started to begin on Thursday night. And then came cocaine . . .

I vividly remember my first impression of the cocaine high: "This isn't spiritual at *all!*" I should have stayed with that line of thinking. It would have saved me so much grief. But, instead, in a fairly rapid fashion, the "spiritual" rationalization of my drug use fell by the wayside. I soon lost my desire for the other chemicals. Cocaine seemed to give me the confidence and energy I increasingly needed to stay atop my growing business and my ever more complex life—but that's just how it *seemed*. In reality, I was becoming addicted. And without knowing it. Addiction is the only disease that tells you you don't have it.

Without going into painful details, my life soon became unmanageable. I violated my own values and the trust of others. I became unreliable, dishonest, and highly preoccupied. I was using to live and living to use. The worst thing was that there seemed to be no end in sight.

And there wasn't, until I entered NA (Narcotics Anonymous). Although I attended mainly to appease my wife, I felt something at that first meeting that sparked some hope—enough to keep me coming back. Here were people with drug-abuse histories as long and sordid as mine (or worse!), who nevertheless were managing to stay clean for impressively long periods of time. Here was a place where you could say anything that was on your mind and people would nod in empathy. NA was shelter from the storm, a place where addicts didn't have to lead miserable, isolated, and dishonest lives. A place where "misfits" could finally fit.

Almost from the beginning, I sensed something wonderfully spiritual about these recovery meetings. For one thing, they were free; nobody was making any money off me. The idea of fellow and sister addicts getting together to help each other was very appealing—and *good* in every sense of that word. People in the program, when they weren't expressing some hurt, anger, pain, or dissatisfaction, appeared genuinely content. And, even when they were expressing pain, it seemed to be accompanied by faith and gratitude.

Most spiritual of all, however, were the Twelve Steps, the guidelines that have functioned as the framework for most of the thousands of self-help groups that now exist. Much has been written about the Twelve Steps elsewhere, and they have been a path to a healthier, happier life for millions of people who have suffered from a wide range of destructive habits or abuse by others, but the main thing to realize is that, regardless of one's particular affliction, the steps offer a *spiritual* approach to the problem. Not a religious one, but a spiritual one.

As a Jew, of course, it is more within my tradition to ask questions than to provide answers. Asking questions is important; it makes us think, it makes us search, it helps us grow. The first question that God asked Adam back in the Garden of Eden, "Where are you?," continues to hang in the air for all eternity. It is a question that echoes within every room of recovery and within every thirsty soul.

Those questions helped me, perhaps forced me, to look for connections between the recovery tradition and the Jewish tradition as I understood them. I found an abundance of such connections. My initial fears that recovery might be incompatible with my particular religious tradition were replaced with the understanding that nothing could be further from the truth. Even better: I found that my continuing growth in recovery was making me a better Jew, and that my Jewish knowledge and background was not harming but actually enriching my recovery. I was experiencing a kind of spiritual synergy, which led me to a feeling of serenity or *shalom*. To have it requires some wisdom and strength, some acceptance and some work, but these blessings are freely available to all who want them. The important thing is to begin . . . and to have faith. As Rabbi Nachman of Bratzlav said, "The entire world is a narrow bridge, but the main thing is not to fear." Let us cross that bridge together. If we but believe it, we are never alone.

AARON Z.

# How To Use This Book

While this book provides the reader with its own unique blend of inspiration and affirmation, it is also a companion to the Torah: the spiritual touchstone of the Jewish people. As a result, its sections follow the traditional cycle of the weekly Torah reading. Just as the Torah is divided into weekly portions so that its entire contents might be read in public over the course of a year, so too is this book designed. However, the Hebrew (soli-lunar) calendar does not precisely follow the secular (solar) calendar. Different adjustments—through double portions—are made each year according to a traditional rabbinic formula.[1] You might want to simply read this book one day at a time, or one week at a time. In that case, begin at the beginning and keep on reading. However, if you choose to use this volume as part of your Torah study and wish to keep in sync with the Jewish world around you, consult the chart on pp. 187–88. This will help you follow the traditional reading for any given calendar year.

Since Torah is read on Mondays and Thursdays, texts have been chosen directly from the Torah portion for these days. The Sunday section as well is introduced by a text from the Torah. Texts from other Jewish sources guide us through the middle of the week. Shabbat frames our week and offers us time for leisurely study. Thus, a Torah text on Friday is used to introduce Shabbat and an inspirational essay emanating directly from the text helps shape our thoughts for this special day.[2] In this volume, both authors' voices are heard during the weekly study of the Torah portion. On Sunday, Tuesday, Wednesday, Friday, and Shabbat, Rabbi Olitzky offers the reader spiritual insights from Jewish tradition. On Mondays and Thursdays, Aaron Z. offers a message from the depths of his experiences in recovery.

---

[1] Each year different portions are doubled in accordance with the holiday schedule, which is fixed by rabbinic formula. In order to approximate a secular year with fifty-two weeks, the portions Tazria and Metzora have been doubled (joined together) in this volume since they often are doubled in the yearly cycle of Torah readings.

[2] Please note that the last Torah portion, Vezot Ha'berachah, is not a regular Shabbat weekly portion. It is reserved for Simchat Torah, at which time the Torah is concluded, rolled back to the beginning and begun once again (with Bereishit). Therefore, the section for Vezot Ha'berachah follows a slightly different format from the rest of the book.

# The Twelve Steps
## of
## Alcoholics Anonymous

The Twelve Steps are reprinted and adapted with permission of Alcoholics Anonymous World Services, Inc. Permission to reprint and adapt the Twelve Steps does not mean that AA is affiliated with the program. AA is a program of recovery from alcoholism—use of the Twelve Steps in connection with programs and activities which are patterned after AA but which address other problems does not imply otherwise.

1. We admitted we were powerless over alcohol—that our lives had become unmanageable.
2. Came to believe that a Power greater than ourselves could restore us to sanity.
3. Made a decision to turn our will and our lives over to the care of God as we understood Him.
4. Made a searching and fearless inventory of ourselves.
5. Admitted to God, to ourselves, and to another human being the exact nature of our wrongs.
6. Were entirely ready to have God remove all these defects of character.
7. Humbly asked Him to remove our shortcomings.
8. Made a list of all persons we had harmed, and became willing to make amends to them all.
9. Made direct amends to such people wherever possible, except when to do so would injure them or others.
10. Continued to take personal inventory and when we were wrong promptly admitted it.
11. Sought through prayer and meditation to improve our conscious contact with God as we understood Him, praying only for knowledge of His will for us and the power to carry that out.
12. Having had a spiritual awakening as a result of these Steps, we tried to carry this message to alcoholics, and to practice these principles in all our affairs.

(The use of the masculine pronoun in referring to God is the original AA language. Like many Twelve Step programs, we have chosen not to use a pronoun at all later in our discussion, but retain the original here.)

*Renewal, like a livelihood, must be earned each day.*

Genesis Rabbah 20:9

# Personal Thoughts and Commitments
## for
## Self-Renewal This Week

# Bereishit: New Beginnings

## Genesis 1:1–6:8

### All beginnings are difficult.
*Mechilta, Yitro 19:5*

- ✔ God brings the world into being, setting it all in order.
- ✔ In the Divine image, God creates the human species, male and female.
- ✔ On the seventh day of Creation, God rests and calls it Shabbat.
- ✔ After they eat from the Tree of Knowledge, God expels the first man and woman from the Paradise of Eden.
- ✔ Cain kills his brother Abel, having decided that God rejected his own sacrifice.
- ✔ Violence fills the earth at the time of Noah.

## Sunday

### And God called to Adam and said to him: *Ayeka?* Where are you?
*Genesis 3:8*

God knows where Adam is and yet calls out after him. It's impossible to really hide from God. *Ayeka:* Hey! Where are *you?*

# Monday

**The serpent beguiled me, and I did eat.**
*Genesis 3:13*

It is no coincidence that the Bible's first recorded incident of human behavior involves succumbing to temptation. The message is universal. It suggests that this is the basic moral challenge that confronts us: the dilemma between doing whatever we want and what is right, between impulse and restraint, between conscience and conceit, between our Higher Power and our lower one. It is all too clear that human beings have it well within their power to get evicted from Paradise almost before their bags are unpacked. A modern commentator sees more than a trace of a Divine "set-up" in the forbidden fruit story and questions whether any person could long resist such an enticing, off-limits tree.

In the grip of active addiction, a compulsively pursued delusion of Paradise eventually becomes a living hell. Curiosity and the thrill of the illicit (not to mention peer-group pressure!) may be common threads linking Adam and Eve's downfall with our own, but the first step in working our way back up is to admit what has happened, that something is wrong in our lives, and that, despite our expert addict excuses and finger-pointing ("the serpent beguiled me") for explaining how it happened, we must be willing to accept responsibility for dealing with it now. Recovery begins with a simple, honest admission: We have a problem, and we need help.

# Tuesday

**The Holy One created everything for
Divine glory.**
*Pirkei Avot 6:11*

We were all fashioned in the image of God. Regardless of what we have done before, each and every one of us carries a spark of the Divine deeply embedded in our souls. We too have the power to create new worlds. All we have to do is to start now.

# Wednesday

**Do not worry about tomorrow's trouble,
for you do not know what the day may
bring. Tomorrow may come and you will
be no more, and so you will have worried
about a world that is not yours.**
*Babylonian Talmud, Yebamot 63b*

Concentrate on today. It is the only day that we can influence. You can work on tomorrow when it gets here.

# *Thursday*

**. . . sin crouches at the door; and unto you
is its desire, but you may rule over it.**
*Genesis 4:7*

This is one of the most poetic descriptions of sin and the dangers that lurk beyond the threshold of our conscience. The evil impulse is shown to be sinister, sneaky, and insidious. It bides its time, waiting for us to slip. Every time we "don't do well," it opens the door a little bit wider. And what it wants is us—its desire is for thee—probably for lunch!

This image of ever-present temptation is particularly relevant to us addicts. We have learned all too painfully what lies outside the door, how our cravings sooner or later turn into a sickness that seems to crave our souls. No matter which step we're on, we are always but a step away . . . the door is never too far away. The good news is that "you may rule over it." Not by ourselves, perhaps, but help is available. All we have to do is ask, and keep asking, and do our best—one day at a time.

Recovery offers us a new beginning and opens up a world of opportunities. Despite temptation's ever-lurking presence, we can have hope today. Together, we can keep our disease at bay.

# *Friday*

**And [Cain] said, "I do not know. Am I my
brother's keeper?"**
*Genesis 4:9*

Responsibility. Whatever you do, you own it. However unpleasant our past deeds may be, we cannot start over until we acknowledge them as our own. Yes, you are your sister's keeper. But be her friend first.

# *Shabbat*

**When God began to create, the world was
gloomy and in disarray. So God sent forth
the Divine spirit, giving it light and order.**
*Genesis 1:1*

The beginning. This is where it all started. No need to look
elsewhere. The rabbis teach us that before God created this
world, God created many others, but unhappy with those ill-
fated attempts, eventually destroyed them. Finally God
rested, satisfied. Ours may not be a perfect world, but it is
the one that God gave us. Our obligation is to make it the
best it can be. What happened before has been absorbed into
a history that no longer exists. The rabbis go so far as to say
that we shouldn't even try to figure out what was wrong with
those prior creations. It's no use. Just begin with the beginning. Begin with today.

Throughout our lives, we are given the chance to begin again.
Every morning, we awaken to a new day, as if it were the
very first. The darkness that enveloped the world during the
night gives way to the dawning of a new day. And we thank
God in our morning prayers that our life has been restored,
that the world has been set in order once again:

> Praised are You, Adonai our God, Ruler of the Universe
> who makes light and forms darkness, who establishes
> peace and is the Creator of all life. With Divine mercy,
> you give light to earth and to all who dwell there. With
> goodness, you renew the work of creation, day by day.
> *From the "Yotzer Or" prayer*

There is an old European Jewish custom that encourages the
renaming of a person during an illness to Chaim or Chaya
(Hebrew for life) to fool the Angel of Death when it is on the
prowl. The past life is forgotten. The person is reborn, emerg-
ing like a newborn babe from the Source of Life itself.

This is the path of recovery. Renewed life, the strength to
begin again.

# Questions for Self-Reflection

1. What am I afraid to begin because it will be so hard?

2. Which temptations do I continue to confront?

3. How can I start over after all these years of doing the same thing?

4. When am I going to finally slow down and really rest my soul?

# Notes to Myself

# Sacred Thoughts for Holy Living

A human being can cut out a form on a wall but cannot make breath, a soul, organs, or intestines for it. But the Holy Blessed One fashions forms within forms, gives them breath, a soul, and all the vital organs needed for life.

*Babylonian Talmud, Megillah 14a*

# For Renewal, A Psalm

Create in me a clean heart, O God

Renew a steadfast spirit in me.

Do not cast me away from Your presence

Nor remove your holy spirit from me.

Return to me the joy of Your deliverance

And let a willing spirit support me.

*Psalm 51:12-14*

# A Prayer

Praised be the One who spoke, and the world came into being. Praised be the Source of all creation. Praised be the One whose words are acts and know no bounds. Praised be the One who has compassion for the earth and all its creatures. Praised be the living God who is the source of our own deliverance and help. With songs of praise, we proclaim you as God, the Source of all life in the universe.

Adapted from *"Baruch She'amar,"*
which introduces *"Pesukei Dezimrah"*
in the morning service

# Personal Thoughts and Commitments
## for
## Self-Renewal This Week

# Noach: Rainbow Covenants

## Genesis 6:9-11:32

**My loyalty shall never move from you, nor my covenant of friendship be shaken.**

*Isaiah 54:10*

- ✔ Noah and his family survive the flood which God uses to cleanse the earth.
- ✔ The rainbow colors the sky and reminds us of God's promise: The world will not be destroyed.
- ✔ The nations who grow out of Noah's surviving family are listed.
- ✔ The Tower of Babel is built and its presumptuous builders are scattered and destined to speak different languages.

## Sunday

**When the bow is in the clouds, I will see it and remember the everlasting covenant between God and all living creatures, all flesh that is on the earth.**

*Genesis 9:15*

Everyone looks for a sign of God's presence. We all want to know that God is with us, wherever we go, whatever we do. The rainbow helps. But look deep inside yourself—you'll find God there, too.

# *Monday*

**I will not again curse the ground any more for humanity's sake . . . neither will I again smite any more every thing living, as I have done.**
*Genesis 8:21*

There are two important recovery messages one can derive from God's "rainbow covenant." One is the fundamental Jewish concern for the sanctity of life. God has every right to destroy God's creation—it belongs to God. Or does it? If the world was created for humankind, and humankind has been given free will, then perhaps it is too severe to make the world's continued existence contingent upon good behavior. There is almost a sense of Divine "letting go" about this.

Perhaps the "rainbow covenant" is nothing less than God's own way of breaking the cycle of global destruction. Perhaps it is God's way of saying, "Live and let live." In our own times, as we appear to be edging back from the abyss of assured mutual destruction, the rainbow serves as a powerful reminder that the best use of power may be in refraining from its use, in turning swords into plowshares, and in preserving life in all its free-willing formats.

The second recovery message is on a personal level. Having survived our own flood, we too can choose to refrain permanently from self-destruction. Our ark is our fellowship, and our rainbow is hope. There will be rainstorms and cloudy days, but there need never again be a flood. We can feel the gratitude of true survivors.

# Tuesday

**There is no sphere in heaven where the soul remains a shorter time than in the sphere of merit; there is none where it abides longer than in the sphere of grace.**

*Baal Shem Tov*

God remembers Noah, but his merit is momentary. It is Divine grace that saves him from the flood. God has promised us as well: As bad as things get, no more floods.

# Wednesday

**The path of the righteous is as the light of dawn, that strives more and more to the perfect day.**

*Proverbs 4:18*

There is nothing haughty about this Noah. "Noah was simply a righteous man" (Genesis 6:9). He is just a simple person. There is a basic goodness about him. Noah does the right thing because he knows it in his heart. His goodness lights the path for others.

# *Thursday*

**And Noah went forth, and his sons, and his wife,
and his son's wives with him . . . out of the ark.**
*Genesis 8:18-19*

As in the first portion of Genesis, the Torah emphasizes the brotherhood and sisterhood of humankind. Adam and Eve are created as the world's first pair, the Midrash tells us, so that everyone's common ancestry will be beyond dispute. Again with Noah, just one family emerges from the ark after the flood. The message is clear: We are family, so why not be a little nicer to each other? The Laws of Noah, part of God's "rainbow covenant," which soon follow in the text, can be seen as yet one more Divine attempt to ensure societal civility. Indeed, one of the recurring themes throughout Genesis is not only how quickly "the sons and daughters of Adam and Eve" forget this basic teaching, but also how even brothers can lose sight of their brotherhood and become lethally estranged.

Addiction cuts across all classes, religions, and ethnic groups. One of the many admirable things about the recovery program is the way it brings together people from all walks of life. At first, some of us may be uncomfortable, or worse, about relating to people of different races, religions, or ethnic origins. But that which brings us together is far stronger than that which would tear us apart. Our Number One reason for being in the program is to help each other. We really do need each other. If we stay open and listen with a willing heart, we will find that we can learn something from everybody. Learning to respect others helps us avoid the pitfalls of inferiority and superiority. In recovery, as in Noah's ark, everyone is in the same boat!

# *Friday*

**And God sent forth a dove . . . but the dove found no rest.**
*Genesis 8:8-9*

All week long, we run around from place to place. Harried, we become weary from life's struggles, the day-to-day affairs of the world. Ah . . . but Shabbat is coming. Rest. Rest. Rest and be renewed.

# *Shabbat*

**This is the sign that I set for the covenant
between Me and you and every living creature
that is with you, for all ages to come.**

*Genesis 9:12*

Covenant. Agreements. Partnerships. God and you. God and me. This is a pivotal point of Jewish life. When we walk with God, as did Noah, we are in good hands, so to speak. But there's more. We too have a responsibility. The rainbow is more than a promise; it is a sign of *our* agreement. No more Babels. No more Sodom and Gomorrah. Only a life that is dedicated to good, clean living. You may not be able to complete the task on your own; that's why you have a partner. You are never alone.

The rainbow is also a multi-colored band of hope: the silver lining to the clouds of destruction that brought the flood. Recovery, too, represents hope, hope that we have found a saner, more spiritual way to live and a guarantee that we never have to return to our past miseries for as long as we live this new way. God's promise to humankind was never again to destroy the whole world. Let recovery be a solemn promise to ourselves: no more self-destruction. No more floods of feel-good remedies. We very nearly drowned. Now we want to live.

You know what you have to do. Just get started and do it. And keep doing it. Once you get going, you won't want to stop.

# *Questions for Self-Reflection*

1. Can I raise myself above the corruption that surrounds me?

2. What will it take to maintain my half of the bargain with God?

3. Do I sometimes value things more than the people I love?

## *Notes to Myself*

# Sacred Thoughts for Holy Living

The difference between the wicked and the righteous is that the wicked are controlled by their hearts and the righteous have their hearts under control.

*Genesis Rabbah 34:10*

# For Renewal, A Psalm

Then they cried unto Adonai in their trouble

And You delivered them out of their distress.

And You led them by a straight way

That they might go to a city of habitation.

Let them give thanks to Adonai for Your mercy

And for Your wonderful works to humankind,

For You have satisfied the longing soul

And the hungry soul You have filled with good.

*Psalm 107:6-9*

# A Prayer

Praised are You, Adonai our God, Master of the Universe, who remembers the covenant, who is faithful to that covenant, and keeps the Divine promise.

*Blessing said on seeing a rainbow*

# Personal Thoughts and Commitments
## for
## Self-Renewal This Week

# Lech Lecha: New Places

## Genesis 12:1-17:27

**Depart out of the earthly matter that encompasses you; escape, man, from the foul prisonhouse, your body, with all your might and main, and from the pleasures and lusts that act as its jailers.**

*Philo of Alexandria*

✔ God calls Abram and tells him to go to the place which will be shown to him.

✔ Caught in the midst of a battle over copper mines, Abram goes out to battle in order to rescue his nephew, Lot, who has been taken as prisoner.

✔ God makes a covenant with Abram in the midst of a sacrifice when God sends forth a flame between the pieces of flesh smoking on the altar.

✔ Ishmael is born to Abram and Hagar, Sarai's maidservant.

✔ Abram is transformed into Abraham as the covenant of circumcision is established as a mark on the flesh.

## Sunday

**And you shall be a blessing.**

*Genesis 12:2*

What a powerful statement! If we change who we are and what we have become to being all that we can be, we have the potential to become a blessing. And in doing all that we can do, God has given us the opportunity to bless others. Go out and share the blessing.

# *Monday*

**Now God said to Abram: "Get yourself out
of your country, and from your birthplace,
and out of your father's house."**
*Genesis 12:1*

The great biblical commentator Rashi (Rabbi Solomon ben Isaac, who lived in Troyes and later in Mainz and Worms in the eleventh century) explains the phrase "get yourself out" as "go for yourself." People enter Twelve Step programs for all sorts of reasons. Some do it to give themselves a temporary break from the treadmill routine of active addiction. Some do it to placate their parents or spouses. Others are ordered by the court into recovery.

Whatever ship brought us here, we are all in the same boat now. We may come into recovery for different reasons, but we stay in recovery for ourselves. The spiritual and emotional growth that recovery brings will surely be of benefit to others, but most of all it is a benefit to ourselves.

The danger in recovering for someone else lies in its conditional nature: What happens when that person is not around? This "I'm-not-here-for-myself" attitude is just another shrewd form of denial.

Recognizing that we are in recovery for ourselves can help strengthen our commitment to the program. The more we *want* to be in recovery, the more we are. It is an interior spiritual journey that we undertake for ourselves.

# Tuesday

**The one who changes one's place
changes one's luck.**
*Jewish folk saying*

It is hard to free oneself of routine, especially when it is so comfortable. Trust in the new direction you set out to look for. It will not elude you if you keep your focus clear. We have to move from where we are. It is the only chance we have to stay alive.

# Wednesday

**Abraham's helper was God. He defeated
the kings with faith rather than force.**
*Genesis Rabbah 28:4*

In this Torah portion, we see one of the few instances in which Abraham is depicted as a warrior. When we realize that he fought with faith, the discord becomes a sweet melody. Listen for it.

# *Thursday*
### Walk before Me and be pure.
*Genesis 17:1*

This is what God says to Abraham while making the covenant. Without too much poetic license, the sentence also could be translated this way: Take steps before Me and be clean.

The Hebrew word for law, *halachah,* also means "the way to walk." The message here is clear. If we remain conscious of the fact that we are always walking before God, it is much easier to be pure. Another definition for sin: behaving as if God weren't there.

Walking also suggests steady spiritual progress—a nice balance between running and standing still (or stagnating). And the Hebrew for the word pure *(tamim)* has a connotation of "whole-hearted," another way of saying that living honestly can keep us spiritually together. Lies and excuses may seem expedient at first, but many of us know too well how living a life of lies can splinter a heart to pieces.

More than any other time of year, it is at the close of Yom Kippur that I feel I am standing before God, forgiven and pure. But it is in the *walking* that we are apt to stumble, even though we never have to hit bottom again. The gates of tears are always open—so, too, the gates of fears. Which way to go? There are certain steps and, when you need it, help on the way. As long as we have faith, new places and challenges will be less daunting. As long as we are walking before God, we are always in the right place.

# *Friday*
### I am a shield to you.
*Genesis 15:1*

We all have different relationships with God. Sometimes where we are and what we are doing forces us to rethink who we are and what we have become, all in relationship to God. Belief comes hard. Faith comes even harder. Begin with little steps. Let God's presence be a shield about you—until you are ready to be a shield for someone else.

# Shabbat

**I will establish my covenant between
Me and you.**
*Genesis 17:2*

Covenants are not made just in body but also in soul. They reach beyond time and space. They connect us with our past and secure our future.

For me, this covenant with God is the gauge by which I measure all that I do: at work, at home. Martin Buber, the great Jewish thinker of the twentieth century, believed that the special relationship one develops with God should be a mirror of all our relationships. He called it "I and Thou." This is quite a challenge: to raise what we do, the way we behave, to heavenly standards. It is especially important now, as we try to reclaim the distance we have created between so many people—those we love, as well as those we hardly know. We may not always be able to realize that goal, but it should be the standard for which we constantly reach, getting closer and closer each time we do. As we get nearer to other people, we get closer to God.

A sentiment often expressed at Twelve Step program meetings is that God works through people. It's true. In very few environments outside of the recovery community can one find people so ready and willing to give of themselves. Rides. Hugs. Support. Love. "Let us love you," the Twelve Step slogan goes, "until you can learn to love yourself." Recovery is, above all, a *we* program. You and me, helping each other, becomes *us*, which, after all, may be just another way of saying, "I and Thou." We take, we give, we pass it on. A covenant for life.

# Questions for Self-Reflection

1. Can I leave it all behind me and set out on a straight path?

2. How will I recognize God's call to me?

## Notes to Myself

# Sacred Thoughts for Holy Living

A person must learn to stand before God.

A person must learn how to walk before God.

A person must learn to pick oneself up after one falls.

What do you do if you feel that you can't pick yourself up? Then you keep on walking and dancing until you dance your way to heaven.

*Rabbi Nachman of Bratzlav*

# For Renewal, A Psalm

Everyone who reveres Adonai is happy

All who walk in Your ways.

When you eat the fruits of your labors

You will be happy and all will be well with you.

*Psalm 128:1-2*

# A Prayer

Adonai, free my mind so that I may follow your ways.

*Ancient Jewish prayer*

# Personal Thoughts and Commitments
# for
# Self-Renewal This Week

# *Vayera: The Challenge of Self*

## *Genesis 18:1-22:24*

## The one who makes the effort to achieve purity will receive Divine assistance toward that goal.

*Babylonian Talmud, Shabbat 104a*

- ✔ Abraham is visited by three Divine messengers. He offers them hospitality, and they promise him a child in his old age.
- ✔ Although the cities are corrupt, Abraham argues for the people of Sodom and Gomorrah to be spared.
- ✔ During his journey to Gerar, Abraham tells its king, Abimelech, that Sarah is his sister, not his wife.
- ✔ Isaac is born, and the line of the patriarchs/matriarchs is continued.
- ✔ Abraham arises early in the morning, takes Isaac with him and gets ready for the sacrifice. An angel intervenes, and the sacrifice of Isaac is averted.

## *Sunday*

**Abraham came forward and said,
"Will You sweep away the innocent
along with the guilty?"**
*Genesis 18:23*

Such moral courage. No need for Abraham to struggle with his conscience. He knows what he has to do, especially in the presence of God. You know what you have to do to set things right. Now just go out and do it. Now. Don't wait. It may be too late.

# Monday

**And Abraham called the name of his son that was born unto him, whom Sarah bore to him, Isaac.**

*Genesis 21:3*

**Now take your son, your only son, whom you love, Isaac, and go to the land of Moriah; and offer him there for a burnt offering.**

*Genesis 22:2*

Both of these portions of the Torah traditionally are read in synagogue during Rosh Hashanah services. Each provides powerful symbols of faith and repentance that get right to the heart of the holiday.

As the world's first person born as a Jew, Isaac is symbolic of the spiritual rebirth that repentance—and recovery—makes possible. We can begin the New Year, or right now, whole-hearted again if we truly regret our past mistakes and put some action where our resolve is: Penitence, prayer, and compassionate acts are the traditional Jewish prescriptions for keeping our consciences serene.

Isaac's birth, coming late in Sarah's life, is nothing short of a miracle. By all conventional wisdom, Isaac should never have been born. As addicts in recovery, we have beaten the odds, too. The good news for Sarah, for addicts, and for anyone wanting to grow spiritually is: It's never too late.

And what of Isaac's narrowly averted sacrifice, one of the most dramatic stories in the Bible? Certainly it establishes that God does not want us to become our own burnt-offerings. But, for me, it suggests the kind of sacrifice that God does want. To do *teshuvah* is to sacrifice our old selves, to let go of past sins, resentments, and mistakes, to cast away the worst part of us and make a heartfelt commitment to our spiritual growth, so that the better part of us may flourish.

As the Lubavitcher Rebbe has said, "You don't have to wait to die to start a new life. In turning to God, [doing *teshuvah*], you can start the next reincarnation right now." Today is always the first day of the rest of our lives. May we live it as well as we can.

# Tuesday

**The world exists only because of
self-restraint in strife.**
*Babylonian Talmud, Hullin 89a*

When things get bad, we have a tendency to strike out at ourselves and at others. Hold back and hug. You've got a lot of
love embedded in your soul. Release all that negative energy.
Share that love with yourself and with others.

# Wednesday

**The pious promise little but do much.**
*Babylonian Talmud, Berachot 60a*

Often we make promises to ourselves. We try to improve
who we are. But we are just human. We try. We fail. We pick
ourselves up and try again. We are what we do. So just do
what you can do. No more. No less. But don't stop. Keep on
doing it.

## *Thursday*
### And after these things, God tested Abraham.
*Genesis 22:1*

Sometimes it takes a cataclysmic event to turn us towards God. As the Baal Shem Tov put it, "Before you can find God, you must lose yourself." Abraham's faith and spiritual level are profoundly ahead of their time, but our tradition tells us, God gives *tzaddikim* (the righteous) harder tests. By being so willing to set aside their selves before the will of God, both Abraham and Isaac demonstrate an awesome level of faith. And God is shown to be a Higher Power who demands a radically different kind of self-sacrifice than the idols who were worshipped in that time.

In *Akedat Yitzchak*, the binding of Isaac, Isaac literally is willing to lay down his life. And Abraham goes against not only every fatherly instinct in his body, as well as his own sense of righteousness, but also against all his preconceptions of what his God wants. That Abraham and Isaac pass this ultimate test of faith dramatically demonstrates two things: one, that Abraham's faith in a righteous God is justified; and two, that God does not want human blood; God wants our hearts.

In the wilderness of our disease, we nearly lost ourselves on the altar of self-destruction. Maybe we had to lose what we lost to find a better way. Maybe people who have wallowed in hopelessness are more amenable to the value of faith. Maybe our test was different. But if we've made it into recovery, we know we have passed.

## *Friday*
### And Abraham named the place Adonai-Yireh, whence the present saying, "On the mount of Adonai, there is vision."
*Genesis 22:14*

Whenever there is an awareness of God's presence, we can see more clearly. All we have to do is open up our eyes. To see ourselves, to see others. And in the reflection, we see God.

# Shabbat

**God said to him, "Abraham," and he
answered, "*Hineini*. Here I am."**

*Genesis 22:1*

While few among us fully understand the sacred drama that
is taking place between God and Abraham as he is asked to
sacrifice Isaac, we do know that Abraham is ready, willing,
and able to respond to God *before* knowing the consequences
of the Divine request.

Here I am. All of me. Everything. Not later, not in a minute.
Right now. Abraham calls out with every fiber of his being;
he knows he needs that strength to stand in God's presence,
to respond to God's call. But he doesn't hesitate, doesn't ask
what God wants. A simple response. "*Hineini*. Here I am for
You." There is nothing half-hearted about *hineini*. Not, "I'll
get back to you," or "Let me check my calendar." It is the
ultimate expression of personal presence.

One rabbi working in recovery told us that *hineini* was a
state of radical readiness. It is the only attitude to have in
recovery, because it is the only one that will work. When it
comes to saving your life, nothing but immediacy will help.

Often, the path in life is not clear. Likewise, in recovery, we
are told things or given suggestions that do not seem to make
sense. At these times, it is good to have a *hineini* attitude. As
one wise friend observed, "The suggestions you get are free.
You only pay if you don't take them." If the willingness is
there, understanding will follow. The closer you are to
answering *hineini*—in life and in recovery—the easier your
journey will be.

# *Questions for Self-Reflection*

1. What does it take to be nice to everyone?

2. Do I have the moral courage to stand up for what I believe—especially in the face of danger?

3. Do I lie to protect myself?

# *Notes to Myself*

# Sacred Thoughts for Holy Living

The one slow to anger is better than the mighty, and the person who controls his passions mightier than the one who conquers a city.

*Proverbs 16:32*

# For Renewal, A Psalm

Into Your hand I commit my spirit,

You have redeemed me, Adonai

O God of truth.

I despise those who regard lying vanities

Instead I trust in Adonai.

I will be glad and rejoice in your loving acts of
    kindness.

For You have seen my affliction.

You have taken cognizance of what troubles my
    soul

And have not given me over into the hand of my
    enemy.

*Psalm 31:6-9*

# A Prayer

Master of the Universe, I hereby forgive all who made me angry and caused me harm, whether they hurt my honor or my property, whether purposely or unwittingly, whether in deed or in thought. May nobody be punished through me or because of me.

*Medieval prayer, an introduction
to the Yom Kippur confessional*

# Personal Thoughts and Commitments
for
## Self-Renewal This Week

# Chayei Sarah: Life Goes On

## Genesis 23:1-25:18

**To everything there is a season and a time to every purpose under Heaven.**

*Ecclesiastes 2:1*

✔ Sarah dies and a grieving Abraham purchases a burial site in the cave of Machpelah.

✔ Life continues, and Isaac betroths Rebecca after she displays such giving qualities at the well.

✔ Then Abraham dies. He too is buried—by his sons Isaac and Ishmael, who have come together after a long separation.

## Sunday

**I am a resident alien among you.**

*Genesis 23:4*

Sarah is dead, and Abraham must find a place to bury her. He feels so far away from home. How often we feel that way. The more desperate our need for home, the further away it seems to be. With God at our side, we are always home.

# *Monday*

## And the life of Sarah was a hundred and seven and twenty years . . .

*· Genesis 23:1*

The Midrash tells us that Sarah always combined in her person the virtues of youth and old age. When she was only twenty, she had the virtues of old age—calmness and moderation. But when she was one hundred years old, she was still blessed with the zeal, vitality, and enthusiasm associated with a young woman.

Being in recovery can, in a spiritual sense, reverse the aging process. We regain our hope, our faith, and our ability to enjoy the simple pleasures of life. We find our "inner child"—that creative, innocent place within us that remains forever young. We start looking better, feeling better, and living better.

Age is relative, and active addiction, whether it involves alcohol, drugs, sex, food, or gambling, has a way of making us old before our time. In recovery, as we learn self-acceptance and become more fully integrated with our past, we are put back in touch with the better parts of ourselves. As we grow, we keep what we need and leave the rest. Who would ever want to forget how to laugh and gurgle (OK, maybe not gurgle) as uninhibitedly as a baby? Or to gaze, full of wonder, at some blazingly colorful fall foliage? And, by the same token, who would want to abandon the lessons and experiences that have made us who we are? Moot question, that. We can't change our past anyway, so we might as well make the most of it.

In recovery, we can have our wisdom and feel good, too. There is no age requirement: just a desire to rid ourselves of old habits that were killing us.

# Tuesday

**Light is perceived only out of darkness.**
*Abraham ben Samuel Halevy ibn Hasdei,*
Ben Ha'melech Ve'hanazir

Even in the worst of times, daily life continues. Jewish tradition beckons us forward—while remaining ever mindful of the past. Abraham knows it. He sends his servant Eliezer to find a wife for Isaac even as the pain of Sarah's death engulfs him. Feeling the presence of God in their midst, they are able to move forward.

# Wednesday

**Fear not; death is not your doom. Remember**
**all that went before and will follow you.**
*Ben Sira 41:5*

Deeds. These accompany us—even to the grave. Know that what you now do will make a difference. People will remember. And you will live.

# Thursday

**And [Laban said to Eliezer]: "Come in . . .
for I have cleared the house."**

*Genesis 24:31*

Rashi's commentary on this line is, "I have cleared the house of idols." In order to let the holy in, we have to be willing to throw the unholy out. Recovery can be thought of as a spiritual "spring-cleaning." Former places, former people, and former things can interfere with our attempts to get on with our lives.

Relics from our past are a bit like idols; they have no inherent power but that which we invest in them. Unfortunately, powerful memories and even urges can be triggered by old playmates and playthings. Having idols in your house does not necessarily make you an idol-worshipper, but it certainly makes it easier to entertain the thought.

It is hard to let go of old ways, even painful ones, but that is what living one day at a time is all about. Abraham illustrates it well. No sooner does he finish mourning for his beloved wife than he gets to the business at hand—negotiating for a burial place. And, then, finding a suitable wife for his son.

That's how to live responsibly: by responding to what has to be done and doing it—one step at a time. Half the trick in mastering life's challenges is simply showing up and being ready. Ambivalent environments foster ambivalent messages. When life comes knocking at our door, are we, like Abraham, ready to say. *"Hineni:* Here I am?"

# Friday

**Isaac went out walking in the field.**

*Genesis 24:23*

Weary from the day, it's good to get out and walk, just to be by ourselves. Sometimes the pressures of life overwhelm us. We need time to think, to sort things out. Or we just need time.

# Shabbat

**Abraham was old, well advanced in years.**
*Genesis 24:1*

The Torah does not instruct us to love our parents, only honor them. It is tempting to play "woulda-coulda-shoulda" with the past, but it is futile. Maybe our parents did the best they could. Maybe they didn't. They are still our parents. Those of us who are parents, who have vowed not to repeat the mistakes of our own parents, have learned how to commit different ones. It may be hard to face, but this realization is a necessary step toward the acceptance of self.

We eventually learn that, despite our efforts to the contrary, we are in large measure like our parents. Especially as adult children, we recognize that we are inextricably bound to one another—parent to child. Indeed, we have *become* them. We all have faced the same chilling revelation. One day we are looking in the mirror, shaving or perhaps putting on makeup. It is early morning, the house is quiet; the sun is just beginning to peek through the stillness of night. And we are alone with our reflection in the mirror, rehearsing the upcoming day's events or thinking about what happened the night before. And then it hits us. We see our father's or mother's face before us in that mirror. Though we may try to struggle free of this image, when we acknowledge it, there is a sense of release, of coming home.

# Questions for Self-Reflection

1. Even if I can leave my past behind me, will I ever be able to forget it?

2. Whom did I push away in my addiction?

# Notes to Myself

# Sacred Thoughts for Holy Living

If God did not conceal from each person the day of death, no one would build a home; and no one would plant a vineyard. Each person would say, "Tomorrow I will die, why should I do all this work for others?" Therefore God concealed the day of a person's death so that that person would build and plant. If we want a long life, then we will enjoy the fruits of labor. If we do not, others will benefit from the work.

*Yalkut Shimoni,* on Ecclesiastes, section 968

# For Renewal, A Psalm

The teaching of Adonai is perfect, renewing life; the decrees of Adonai are enduring, making wise the simple,

The precepts of Adonai are just, rejoicing the heart; the instruction of Adonai is clear, giving light to the eyes.

The fear of Adonai is pure, abiding forever; the judgements of Adonai are true, they are harmonious altogether.

They are more desirable than gold, yes, than very fine gold; sweeter than honey, or drippings of honeycomb.

Your servant pays them heed; in obeying them there is much reward. Who can be sure of errors? Clear me of hidden guilt.

Keep your servant from presumptuous sins; let them not dominate me; then shall I be blameless and clear of transgression.

*Psalm 19:8-14*

# A Prayer

I pray that I may be forgiven for anything I said or did to you, for any moment of discomfort or pain I ever caused you. Forgive me for any thoughtless or selfish act, for any sin, intentional or unintentional, toward you. Before God I swear that I bear no ill will for any wrong which you may have committed against me.

May I recall all that was good and noble in your life so that it might inspire me to walk in the way of righteousness, to be kind to all those I encounter on the path of life.

*From the graveside prayer for forgiveness*

# Personal Thoughts and Commitments
## for
## Self-Renewal This Week

# Toldot: Family Baggage

## Genesis 25:19-28:9

**There are three partners in the creation of a life: mother, father, and God.**

*Babylonian Talmud, Kiddushin 30b*

✔ Jacob and Esau struggle in Rebecca's womb before birth.

✔ Famished, Esau sells his birthright legacy as a firstborn to his younger brother for a mess of potage.

✔ Isaac repeats the actions of his father in pretending that Rebecca is his sister, not his wife.

✔ Conspiring with his mother, Jacob tricks Isaac into bestowing upon him the blessing originally intended for Esau.

✔ Fearing that Esau will kill him, Jacob flees for his life.

## Sunday

**If so, why do I exist?**

*Genesis 25:22*

Rebecca is pained by the struggle of her sons while they are still in the womb. Whether as young children or adults, we often bear the burden of our children's (and parents') struggle with themselves, with one another, and with us. Just let go. There is nothing else you can do.

# *Monday*

**And [Esau] ate and drank, and rose
up and went his way, and Esau
despised his birthright.**

*Genesis 25:34*

The birthright is a purely spiritual inheritance, indicating who would succeed as the head of the clan in priestly activities. It is this spiritual legacy that Esau values less than a bowl of hot lentil soup.

Jacob cannot be excused for deceiving his brother, although many biblical commentators have exerted considerable mental effort and ink trying. But neither can Esau be let off the hook for regarding his birthright so lightly.

No, it seems that in this episode there is plenty of shoddy behavior to go around. Each seems all too ready to take advantage of each other's weakness and character defects: Esau's physical hunger and Jacob's spiritual neediness. One is too gruff, and the other too sly.

In unhealthy relationships, that's often the way it is—people taking advantage of each other. In healthier ones, mutual caring and sharing replaces mutual exploitation. When we stop trying to compete with each other, the relationship paradigm goes from win-lose to win-win.

This truth is one that seems to have eluded Jacob and Esau, but it doesn't have to escape us. Open, honest, caring relationships become more possible in recovery, perhaps for the first time. It becomes easier to accept others as we learn to accept ourselves. After all, none of us is without shortcomings. Keeping that in mind can keep us humble. And doing the best we can to help others can keep us clean.

# Tuesday

**When an offender receives a penalty, he
becomes your brother.**

*Babylonian Talmud, Megillah 7b*

Jacob and Esau never quite understood this notion. Esau was
ready to give up his birthright for a bit of food, and Jacob
was ready to receive it. Eventually, they would become
reunited at their father's gravesite. Don't wait for more pain
to bring your family together. You've suffered enough. It's
time to become brothers and sisters once again.

# Wednesday

**As my ancestors planted for me, so do I
plant for my children.**

*Babylonian Talmud, Taanit 23a*

In the depths of addiction, you may not have seen so clearly
the tree which your parents or those who came before you
planted on your behalf. But its roots have clung to the soil for
life, sustained and nurtured even amidst fierce winds. Take a
sapling in your hand and plant it. Then go wait for the messianic era to come.

# *Thursday*

**And the children struggled together within her.**
*Genesis 25:22*

Less than the thinness of a membrane separated Esau and Jacob in the womb, yet their struggle, we are told, begins even then. Sometimes, the familiarity and close quarters of family life can breed contempt. Even in the most loving families, we often suffer from a variety of emotional bumps and bruises that can take a long time to heal. Real life is not *Ozzie and Harriet,* or even *All in the Family.* There is jealousy, competition, insecurity, and favoritism. There is even alcoholism, denial, violence, and abuse—problems that don't get resolved after the commercial.

Some intrafamily relationships are closer than others. Some just never seem to work—no matter how hard we try.

As children, many of us learned to cope as best we could with dysfunctional families. But not only is developing a healthy identity unlikely in an unhealthy family, it's also hard to learn anywhere else. So as adults we must learn to forgive ourselves for past damage—that which we did and that which was done to us. We must let old wounds heal.

Yes, Isaac loved Esau more, and Rebecca loved Jacob more, and maybe that was wrong. But it's also the way it was. In forgiving others, we learn to forgive ourselves. You can't hold onto your brother's heel—or family baggage—forever. To do so becomes a self-inflicted handicap, like going through life with one hand tied behind your back. There comes a time for letting go. Let that time be now.

# *Friday*

**We have found water.**
*Genesis 26:32*

The life-giving waters of repentance and return nourish our spirit and our soul. Don't depend on others. Go out and find the water for yourself.

# Shabbat

**Isaac dug anew the water wells . . . and he
gave them the same names that his father
had given them.**

*Genesis 26:18*

Isaac searches for the wells. He yearns for the redemptive power they may unleash for him, as they did for his father. Isaac has journeyed far from his roots. Here at the wells he returns to his source. In the midst of what begins as another expulsion, he redigs the exact same wells as had Abraham and gives them the exact same names as had Abraham. Isaac finds waters in these wells—saving waters. Saving waters which his father, Abraham, had in a sense stored up for him before, just as our parents have done for us. Isaac has to dig through exactly what Abraham had to dig through, in order to uncover his own essence once again. It is only after Isaac works through the vulgar day that he is able to call the wells by the same names as Abraham had. His former life is eclipsed at that moment. Not only does he dig deeply into the earth but, in doing so, he also digs deeply into himself.

# Questions for Self-Reflection

1. What can I do to avoid being desperate enough to sell my birthright?

2. How do I continue to deceive those whom I love?

3. What in my family's past have I yet to work through on my own?

# Notes to Myself

# Sacred Thoughts for Holy Living

Rabbi Judah ben Shulam told of a king's son who was anxious that everyone should know that he was a prince. "Oh my father," he once cried, "let the people know that I am the king's son." "Would you have the people know that are you my son?" asked the king. "Then don my regal robe and put on my crown and let the people see with what grace and honor you wear them."

*Deuteronomy Rabbah 7:10*

# For Renewal, A Psalm

Do not hide Your face from me,
Do not cast me out in anger.
You have been my help.
Do not send me away or forsake me
O God of my deliverance.
Though my mother and father abandon me,
Adonai will take me in.

*Psalm 27:9-10*

# A Prayer

We thank You, O God, for our family and for what we mean and bring to one another. We are grateful for the bonds of loyalty and affection which sustain us and for the capacity to love and to care.

Help us to be modest in our demands of one another, but generous in our giving to each other. Keep us gentle in our speech. When we offer words of criticism, may they be chosen with care and spoken softly. May we waste no opportunity to speak words of sympathy, of appreciation, of praise.

Bless our family with health, happiness, and contentment. Above all, grant us the wisdom to build a joyous and peaceful home in which Your spirit will always abide.

*Adapted from* Likrat Shabbat
*by Sidney Greenberg*
*Bridgeport, CT: The Prayer Book Press, 1973*

# Personal Thoughts and Commitments
## for
## Self-Renewal This Week

# Vayetze: Dreams
## Genesis 28:10–32:3

**How awesome is this place! This is none other than the abode of God, and that is the gateway to heaven.**
*Genesis 28:17*

✔ Fleeing Esau, Jacob stops on his way to Haran. There he dreams of a ladder extending to heaven with angels ascending and descending.

✔ In Haran, Jacob is deceived by Laban, who marries him to Leah before allowing him to marry Rachel.

✔ Both wives give birth—Leah to six sons and a daughter and Rachel to Joseph.

✔ Afraid of Laban, Jacob flees once again, this time with his family and all their belongings, including the household gods that Rachel has taken.

## Sunday
**If God remains with me . . .**
*Genesis 28:21*

Deals. Always making deals. If you do this, then I will do that. Enough already. No more deals! Just stay clean.

# Monday

**And Jacob awoke from his sleep . . .
and he was afraid.**
*Genesis 28:16-17*

Dreams about the things we once craved can be disturbing. Graphically and emotionally vivid, they provide a too-close-for-comfort simulation of active addiction with all of its thrill and guilt and shame.

Except that such dreams are not real and are truly beyond our control. They simply indicate a memory or a wish or a desire to use on the subconscious level, which is hardly surprising, given the strong hold alcohol, food, sex, drugs—all the substances we have craved—have had on our minds even during waking states.

But they're only dreams, memories that refuse to fade. They don't mean that your recovery is slipping. They are not prophetic. And they are nothing to be ashamed of. Think of them as urges in your sleep.

When you think about it, these urges have played such a significant role in our lives that it would be unusual not to have them. But they are uncomfortable and weird (perhaps even pleasant) enough by themselves without our having to feel bad for having them. Having a nightmare doesn't mean that you're a monster.

Perhaps the "silver lining" of these dreams is that they give us just one more reason to be grateful for waking up another day in recovery.

# Tuesday

**The great quality of the Jews is that they
have been able to dream through all the
hazards during centuries; and mankind has
credited them with another quality, the
power to realize their dream.**

*Louis D. Brandeis*

Realize your dreams. The power to do so lies deep within you. You'll find it. Just reach in.

# Wednesday

**Im tirtzu, ein zo aggadah.
If you really want it, it is no dream.**

*Theodor Herzl*

Herzl dreamt of a homeland for the Jewish people. Not an easy dream, but one that kept our people alive. It took years. He did not live to see it. It is still taking years. Keep on dreaming and work toward making your dream—your sobriety—real.

# *Thursday*

**And he dreamed and beheld a ladder . . . and the angels of
God ascending and descending on it.**
*Genesis 28:12*

Jacob's famous dream, of angels ascending and descending
the ladder to heaven, recalls this powerful Hasidic teaching:
"When is the man lower on the ladder higher than the man
who is higher on the ladder? When the lower one is climbing
up and the higher one is descending down." Steps up and
steps down, progress and setbacks seem to characterize our
approach to our Higher Power. Some days we are closer than
others. Some nights we have tossed and turned on our own
pillows of stone.

On other nights, beneath a canopy of twinkling stars, we
realize along with Jacob that there is no place where God is
not. Even on that hard pillow. For us in recovery, there are
Twelve Steps on the ladder, guardian angels (sponsors), and
an awakened realization that the Divine Presence permeates
the world.

But the Hasidic parable also tells us that recovery can be
measured by the direction it moves in. Are you headed for the
door or coming back for more? We who are in recovery are
all equally close to that next drink or drug or quick-fix-of-
choice. As the Zohar, the essential text of Jewish mysticism,
puts it, "In truth, a person by her actions is always drawing
to herself . . . good or evil, according to the path which she
treads."

Where we are "is right where we are supposed to be," asserts
a program slogan. But where we are going is up to us.

# *Friday*

**You are truly my bone and flesh.**
*Genesis 29:14*

This is connecting. We don't feel this close to others often
enough. And that's what it's all about. Being at one with
another.

# Shabbat

**God was in this place and I didn't know it.**
*Genesis 28:16*

Jacob goes to sleep without knowing that the very spot on which he rests has been designated as the "gateway to heaven." In fact, the Midrash conflates this spot with Moriah, the place where God is revealed to Abraham after the binding of Isaac and which later becomes the site of the Jerusalem Temple.

The place is sacred; it is where heaven and earth meet, the axis around which Jews are to structure space.

But the Hebrew text includes an apparently superfluous word, the repetition of *anochi*, the emphatic Hebrew word for "I." Why *anochi*? Why not the less emphatic *ani* or, better yet, no explicit pronoun at all? In Hebrew, the subject pronoun is implied in the suffix of the verb *yadati* ("I did . . . know"). The plain or literal sense of the statement would have been amply clear without the extra word *anochi*.

This extra "I" serves, then, as the opening wedge for the wealth of midrashic interpretations which the verse has evoked.

First the broader context. We know from the previous chapters of the text that Jacob has manipulated his brother out of his birthright. We also know that Jacob has conspired with his mother to deceive his father and to rob his brother of their father's blessing. While Jacob may be going to Haran to find a wife, he is also escaping his brother's wrath and fleeing for his life. As Esau complained, the name "Jacob," literally, "the supplanter" (Genesis 27:36), is well deserved.

Against this background, Jacob dreams his dream. With a modicum of homiletic stretching, I suggest we read his reaction this way: "Surely God is in this place! But am I? *(va'anochi?)* That, I don't know! *(lo yadati!)."*

This reading captures the ambivalence that lies at the heart of Jacob's character from the outset and throughout his entire story.

It also suggests that Jacob has a dawning awareness of the ambiguities in his own character. He awakens from his dream and suddenly realizes that he has been designated as the heir to God's promises to Abraham and Isaac.

But he is far from sure that he is ready for that role. Thus, his reaction: God may very well be here, in this place, ready to meet me and to commit to me. But am I? Am I really here? Am I ready for this charge? Am I the person I should be?

*Rabbi Neil Gillman*

## Questions for Self-Reflection

1. What can I do to retrace the steps I have taken away from my family and friends?

2. Whom do I continue to deceive?

3. Why do I still try to run away from who I am?

## Notes to Myself

# Sacred Thoughts for Holy Living

A young man told the Rabbi of Rizhyn that he needed God's help in breaking the evil impulse. The rabbi's eyes laughed as he looked at him: "Are you dreaming? You want to break impulses? You will break your back and your hip, yet you will not break an impulse. But if you pray and learn and work in all seriousness, the evil in your impulses will vanish of itself."

# For Renewal, A Psalm

When Adonai restores the fortunes of Zion
   —we see it in our dreams—
   our mouths will be filled with laughter
   our tongues, with songs of joy.
Then shall they say among the nations,
   "Adonai has done great things for them!"
Adonai will do great things for us
   and we shall rejoice.

*Psalm 126:1-3*

# A Prayer

Master of the Universe, I do not beg You to reveal to me the secret of Your ways—I could not bear it! But show me one thing. Show it to me more clearly and more deeply. Show me what is happening at this very moment, what it means to me, what it demands of me, what You, Master of the Universe, are telling me through it. It is not why I suffer that I want to know, but only whether I suffer for You.

*Rabbi Levi Yitzchak of Berditchev*

# Personal Thoughts and Commitments
## for
## Self-Renewal This Week

# Vayishlach: Struggling with Self

## Genesis 32:4-36:43

**Two drives beat within one person.
One brings health and the other disease.
The strong one wins.**

*Tikkunei Zohar 151a*

✔ Jacob's exile is finally ended. Preparing to reconcile with Esau, he stops for the night. There Jacob wrestles with God and with self and emerges in the morning as Israel.

✔ Jacob's family confronts the pain and humiliation of the rape of Dinah.

✔ Rachel dies, and Esau's family grows.

## Sunday

**If I appease him with gifts in advance, then face him, perhaps he will show me favor.**

*Genesis 32:21*

Forget all those "I'm sorry" gifts. They don't change anything. Such "stinking thinking." We simply have to face each deceit of the past. Change what happened by changing what is happening now.

# Monday

**And Jacob struggled with a stranger all
night. . . . Then the stranger said, "Let me
go, for dawn is breaking." But Jacob
answered, "I will not let you go, unless
you bless me."**
*Genesis 32:25-27*

Some commentators see the stranger as an angel. Others see
him as the stranger within, the part of us that says it's OK to
deceive others, to cut corners, and to taste forbidden fruit.
There is something sinister about this angel/demon. He and
Joseph fight wordlessly through the night. It is only when
dawn is about to arrive that the stranger says, "Let me go," as
if he can not tolerate the light of day. The dark side never can.

We have spent many a night battling our own demons, and
despite the insanity of it all, we know how hard it is to let go.
Perhaps, like Jacob, we need to know that something good
will come from it all. We want a blessing. Recovery is that
blessing, as it helps us choose life and returns us to the Source
of all blessing.

As his blessing, Jacob's name is changed to Israel. In recovery,
we gain a new identity too: My name is _____, and I'm an
alcoholic, compulsive gambler, overeater, or addict. The road
to recovery begins when we acknowledge who we are. It is
easier for us to make this admission now, because we finally
are doing something about it. For us, the struggle of "using
to live and living to use" is over. We didn't quit, we surren-
dered. Thank God!

# Tuesday

**God's Holy Spirit suffuses only hearts that
are joyous.**
*Jerusalem Talmud, Sukkot 5:1*

It is not easy to transcend all of the pain we have caused others and caused ourselves. We carry those memories forward into time. But stop dwelling on the hurt. Adjust your focus. Look at the new happiness you have found in sobriety. Your life is full of potential joy yet to be tasted.

# Wednesday

**After you have paid your fine in court, sing
a song and walk away.**
*Babylonian Talmud, Baba Kamma*

When the struggle is over, forget about it. It's done. Be gone with it. Stop fighting with yourself. Just let it go.

# *Thursday*

**And he said: "Your name shall no more be Jacob, but Israel, for you have struggled with God and with men and have prevailed."** *Genesis 32:29*

By the waters of the Jabbok River, whose very sound is like Jacob twisted around a bit, Jacob silently struggles with his adversary through the night. His new name, Israel, means "he who has struggled with God." The odd thing is that Jacob's new name is not consistently used afterward. For the most part, he remains Jacob. Even in the thrice-daily "Amidah" prayer, we, "the children of Israel," pray to "the God of Jacob."

What kind of a name change is this? Perhaps an internal one—a struggle for identity. A struggle that goes back to the womb, when Jacob cannot keep Esau from being born first, and continues through his conniving his brother out of the firstborn's blessing. But tonight, on the eve of this fateful (and possibly fatal) rendezvous with Esau, it is time to stop running. Time to take a stand. Time to get painfully honest about who Jacob is and why he is here. Time to accept.

When we fight ourselves, the result is always the same: a tie. You can't fight yourself and win. Every addict knows that. On the other hand, a tie against God is nothing to sneeze at. It is, in a way, the quintessential Jewish approach to life: We struggle, we fight, we ask questions, and then *maybe* we reach some kind of better understanding. The struggle to find ourselves can leave us emotionally limping. But sooner or later in recovery, we get strong enough and honest enough with ourselves to be able to accept all the aspects of our identities—the good and the bad. And then we no longer have to fight or pretend. We know who and what we are, and it doesn't really matter what anybody calls us. We have learned what to call ourselves.

# *Friday*

**Jacob kept silent.** *Genesis 34:6*

Speak up. Tell yourself and tell others. When one of us is hurt, we all bleed. Be silent no more. We have much work to do. Hurry.

# Shabbat

**Rid yourselves of the alien god in your midst, purify
yourselves and change your clothes.**
*Genesis 35:2*

How can something as trivial as changing our clothes have
anything to do with ridding ourselves of an alien god? The
alien god is actually the dark, sick part of ourselves. In order
to neutralize it, we have to change. Clothing seems superfi-
cial. But such small acts can pave the way to a major change
of heart. As for purifying ourselves, Judaism provides us a
precious opportunity every week.

There is no better word to describe it than "Shabbat," or
maybe "Shabbos," that time we yearn for all week long,
when the struggle is over—if only for twenty-four hours.
Tasting Shabbat, we taste what is possible when we won't
have to fight with ourselves any longer. God takes over for a
while to remind us who's who and what's what. But reality
warns us. There is still much work to be done if we are to
return fully to the us that God created. For we have but one
God. The chemicals that we worshipped, the food that
bowed us low, the sex that we idolized—none can fill our
souls and set us free. It takes time to realize, but we are finally here—clean and full of Shabbat.

Now go and change your clothes. The messianic banquet is
about to begin, and you're the guest of honor. We all are.

# Questions for Self-Reflection

1. What need I do to end my exile?

2. With whom should I reconcile and make amends?

3. What name should I call myself now?

## Notes to Myself

# Sacred Thoughts for Holy Living

Do not fault another person for a shortcoming that you your-self have.

*Babylonian Talmud, Baba Metzia 59b*

# For Renewal, a Psalm

To You, O God, do I lift my soul

In You, have I trusted.

The troubles of my heart have grown

O bring me out of my distresses.

Be my affliction and my travail

And forgive all my sins.

*Psalm 25:1-2, 17-18*

# A Prayer

Bend our will so that we may submit to You.

*Babylonian Talmud, Berachot 60b*

# Personal Thoughts and Commitments
## for
## Self-Renewal This Week

# Vayeshev:
# Handling Resentments
## Genesis 37:1-40:23

**Great is the person who ignores his own dignity and is not angered by affronts.**
*Midrash Gadol Ve'gedolah 15*

- ✔ Young Joseph dreams of superiority.
- ✔ Joseph's father gives him an ornamented tunic.
- ✔ Joseph is sold to the Midianites.
- ✔ Playing the harlot, Tamar tricks Judah into lying with her.
- ✔ Joseph, now in Egypt, is made head of Potiphar's house—until he refuses to lie with his wife.

# Sunday

**Let's kill him and throw him into one of the pits.**
*Genesis 37:20*

That's one way of handling resentments, but not the right way. It's such negative energy. Why not harness it and make it do good instead? Force yourself until it comes freely.

# *Monday*

**After a time, his master's wife cast her
eyes upon Joseph; and she said, "Lie with
me." But he refused.**

*Genesis 39:7-8*

In the cabalistic cosmology, most of the ten *sefirot* (Divine
emanations, holy crowns, spiritual channels) are symbolized
by biblical figures. The one who symbolizes *Yesod*, or sexual/
life energy, is Joseph. His encounter with Mrs. Potiphar is
probably the reason why. When this portion is chanted in synagogues, the musical note for the Hebrew word for "But he
refused" is a rare one. Called a *shalshelet*, it only occurs four
times throughout the Torah. It is a note that wavers back and
forth, tremulously, about four times. In this context, it suggests profound ambivalence and conflict within Joseph. He
knows what's right, but he also knows what's right in front of
him. The bottom line, though, is that he resists.

He is propositioned again and he resists again—although this
time he has to flee. Thus, Joseph becomes the symbolic
essence of sexual energy—not because of his many conquests,
but because he does the right thing, even in the face of serious
temptation.

Mrs. Potiphar, on the other hand, does not take rejection
well. Her false charges cause Joseph to be thrown in jail. The
recovery lesson here may be this: We can't control what other
people think of us or want from us. We may even suffer as a
result. We do have control, however, over our own expectations. And, what may seem a very reasonable expectation to
us, may not seem so to others. But reasonable or unreason-
able, expectations are just expectations. They are by no
means our due. What's certain, though, is that the more of
them we have, the more likely that we are going to be disap-
pointed. And, too often, disappointment leads to resentment
and sick attempts at revenge. When you are next tempted,
and you will be, sing out your *shalshelet* loud and clear!

# Tuesday

**The Divine attribute which encourages
goodness exceeds the attribute which
sends punishment.**

*Babylonian Talmud, Yoma 46a*

It takes great courage for Judah to admit his error—even after he had been so cleverly reminded by Tamar. He says, "She is more right than I" (Genesis 38:26). You'll know that you've handled a resentment when you too can say, "Well, maybe she was right,"—and that means, "Maybe I was wrong."

# Wednesday

**If there is bitterness in the heart, even sugar
in the mouth won't make life sweeter.**

*Yiddish proverb*

Every day, we face resentments and choices. We either can let things go and move on or we can let them fester, until they poison everything we say or do. Say you don't care about what happened *and* mean it.

# *Thursday*

## Now Israel loved Joseph more than all his children . . .

### *Genesis 37:3*

The Talmud (Shabbat 10b) teaches, "One should never show favoritism among one's children, for because of two coins' worth of fine wool that Jacob gave to Joseph beyond what he gave to the other sons, the brothers became jealous, and one thing led to another until our ancestors became slaves in Egypt." In more ways than one do resentment and jealousy lead down the road to slavery. They fester in our soul, leaving us feeling shortchanged, deprived, and "less than." Left unchecked, this seething anger can explode into vicious acts of reprisal. We can justify almost anything, if we feel we have been gravely wronged.

In truth, there always are going to be people with more and less than what we have. But feeling sorry about what we don't have is counterproductive to our recovery. Being satisfied is not about what one has or doesn't have. It's about learning to appreciate what one has. And it's about choosing life, too, because resentment is a slow, simmering form of self-destruction.

Admittedly, Joseph is more than a little arrogant and quite insensitive to his brothers' feelings. Nevertheless, their reaction, like most envy-driven behavior, is ugly, brutal, and drastic. Eventually, they regret the misery it brings their father. Eventually, the two sides hug. But how many years have been needlessly lost?

The Torah tells us that we are all rich if we are but satisfied with our portion. The best way to avoid resentment is to pursue gratitude. But what of the inevitable resentments that won't let go? We can share them in meetings and with trusted friends or therapists, we can pray that they be removed, and we can have faith that eventually they will. Keep in mind that the person most harmed by a resentment is the one who harbors it.

# *Friday*

## But even while he was in prison, Adonai was with Joseph.

### *Genesis 39:20-21*

Although he has been wronged, Joseph stands his ground. True, he ends up in jail. But Adonai stays with him. Often, we make prisons out of our own souls, but, even then, God is with us.

# Shabbat

**Think of me when all is well with you again and do
me the kindness of mentioning me to Pharaoh so as to
free me from this place. For in truth, I was kidnapped
in the land of the Hebrews and have done nothing
that they should have put me in the dungeon.**

*Genesis 40:14-15*

Instead of letting hate build up inside of him, Joseph, even
while in prison, continues to live the life he has always lived.
Or does he? Gone is the childhood flaunting of his perceived
superiority. There are no more favorite coats or favorite sons.
He harbors no ill will toward his brothers or toward
Potiphar. In prison, he has shed his former self. As others
gain freedom before him, he asks one thing: Just remember
me for who I am.

That's all we can really ask for—to be remembered for who
we are. So shape up. Be what you want remembered. Our
tradition tells of a king who was distressed because his young
child had scratched his favorite diamond. Experts were called
in. No one could repair the damage. And all were afraid that
they would make it worse. An unknown artisan appeared.
Unafraid, he took his tools in hand and deliberately turned
the scratch into a lovely seven-petaled rose.

# Questions for Self-Reflection

1. What can I do to prevent the building of my own self-esteem at the expense of others?

2. Have I faced up to my responsibilities—even amidst the fear of failure?

3. How have I acted to imprison myself?

# Notes to Myself

# Sacred Thoughts for Holy Living

The one who is learned in Torah but does not have the fear of God before his eyes is like a treasurer who possesses the keys of the inner doors but lacks the keys to the outer door. How will he endure?

*Babylonian Talmud, Shabbat 31a*

# For Renewal, a Psalm

Adonai, how numerous have my enemies become
How many are those who have risen up against me
So many that say that there is no redemption for
   me in God.
But You O God are a shield about me
My glory and the one who lifts up my heart.
With my voice I call out to Adonai
And You answer me out of Your holy mountain.

*Psalm 3:1-5*

# A Prayer

Cast all the sins of Your people, the house of Israel, into a place where they will be no longer remembered or ever again come to mind.

*From the "Tashlich" ceremony of Rosh Hashanah*

# Personal Thoughts and Commitments
## for
## Self-Renewal This Week

# Miketz: Destiny

## Genesis 41:1-44:17

**My feet lead me to the place I love.**

*Babylonian Talmud, Sukkah 53a*

✔ Joseph is called out of prison to interpret the dreams of Pharaoh.

✔ In appreciation, Pharaoh appoints Joseph as vizier, in charge of the food supply during the years of plenty and the years of famine.

✔ Joseph's brothers go down to Egypt to get food, for the famine has struck Canaan, as well.

✔ Holding Simon as ransom, Joseph sends the brothers back to Canaan to fetch Benjamin.

✔ The brothers return to Egypt. There, Joseph frames them by placing his own goblet in Benjamin's sack.

## Sunday

**Not I, God will see to Pharaoh's welfare.**

*Genesis 41:16*

A reminder. Joseph is not in control. Like all of us, he is merely a vessel through which God's holiness flows into the world. No, not merely! For God has created us only a little less than Divine.

# Monday

**And behold, seven other cows came up after them . . . and stood by the other cows . . . and the [lean] cows ate up the seven well-favored and fat ones.**

*Genesis 41:3-4*

One commentator sees the cows of Pharaoh's dream as being symbolic of the evil urge: "The evil urge begins like a guest and proceeds like the host." At first, the lean cows merely walk up to the fat ones, slowly and innocuously. Then, they stand by the fat cows, a bit more boldly, but still without any overt harmful intent. Finally, the fat cows are fully consumed. Unless we do something about it.

Addiction is a lot like that: We don't see it coming until it's almost too late. What starts out as harmless good fun eventually gets sought more desperately, more compulsively. The "guest" takes over and almost eats us alive.

The hopelessness and despair we feel in the throes of this disease can be chemically related, but we can't learn that until we stop. We may feel a certain inevitability about the whole thing: Perhaps we were meant to suffer.

Well, that isn't the first time we've been wrong! Rehabilitation can help us turn that kind of fatal thinking around. The disease can be arrested. A whole bunch of good people are proving that every day. I hope today that you're one of them.

# Tuesday

**If a tribulation befalls a person, let him not cry out to Michael or Gabriel, but only to God.**
*Jerusalem Talmud, 9:1*

Joseph follows this advice. He acknowledges God's place in his life. Joseph's brothers cry out, "What is this that God has done to us?" (Genesis 42:28). God has kept you alive. That's what. After all, you have done . . . and deserved. So don't dwell on your own pain. Others are not quite as fortunate as you. They are already dead. You have to work at it to stay alive. It's all up to you—and God, of course.

# Wednesday

**There is nothing more futile than to learn and not to teach.**
*Ecclesiastes Rabbah 5:9*

Joseph teaches Pharaoh and those in his court. Everyone needs a teacher, a sponsor. No one is too young to teach or too old to learn. Remember, we are all going in the same direction. If you aren't, you're going the wrong way.

# *Thursday*

**Jacob saw that there was corn in Egypt and Jacob said to his sons: "Why do you look at one another?"**
*Genesis 42:1*

Joseph could have become embittered and paralyzed by despair at being sold into slavery by his brothers. He is not. He could have been broken by the false sexual harassment charge that sent him to prison for twelve years. He is not. And he could have taken revenge on his brothers. Which he does do, a little, by making his brothers squirm, but if there's one thing the Torah is good at teaching, it's that nobody's perfect.

The point is that Joseph does not despair or bemoan his fate. He accepts what happens to him and does the best he can in whatever situation he is in. With serenity and faith.

Sometimes our destiny—or God's plan—is difficult to accept. As a Yiddish proverb puts it, "God gave burdens, also shoulders." And friends and families and prayers and time to heal. Dealing with life as best we can is what recovery is all about. Some days *will* be painful. But there will be growth and support and days of joy, too. And a Higher Power to turn to.

# *Friday*

**Go back in peace.**
*Genesis 44:17*

A father's blessing to his sons. What more can Jacob request? Go toward peace. Work for it. It is the ultimate state of being, inside and out.

# Shabbat

**Do this and you shall live.**
*Genesis 42:18*

Do this, and I will live. Sounds pretty simple. Now, all I have to do is figure out what "this" is. It's really easier than you think. But you have to look for the answers, chase after them. They are not going to come chasing after you. Rabbi Judah ben Asher tells of a wicked man who committed all kinds of sins. One day, he asked a wise man to teach him an easy way to repent. The wise man said, "Refrain from telling lies." That's a start. Begin the process. Stop lying to yourself. Be brutally frank. We know it hurts. We all see ourselves in your reflection. It stings; it burns. We don't want to kid you. It never really gets any easier; you just get better at it.

Then, stop lying to everyone else. Pave a path for truth. The Psalmist said, "Light is sown for the righteous" (Psalm 97:1). Let truth illumine your path in life. It will get you to where you want to go. And beyond.

The Twelve Steps provide a basic life plan which anybody can use. Torah teaches us how to live that life.

# Questions for Self-Reflection

1. What will release me from my prison?

2. Where can I go to find nourishment for those I love?

3. What provisions can I make to prevent a return to Egypt?

# Notes to Myself

# Sacred Thoughts for Holy Living

Do not run too far, for you must return the same distance.

*Kohelet Rabbah 11, 1*

# For Renewal, A Psalm

I have always set Adonai beside me
Surely You are at my right hand
I shall not be moved.
Therefore, my heart is glad and my glory rejoices
My flesh safely dwells.
For You will not abandon me to the netherworld
Nor will You force the righteous one to suffer
 and see the pit.
You make me know the path of life.
In Your presence is fullness of joy, in Your right
 hand is eternal bliss.

*Psalm 16:8-11*

# A Prayer

O God who is gracious and full of mercy, slow to anger and abounding in loving acts of kindness, I confess to You with a broken and contrite heart that I have sinned and have done evil in Your sight. Behold, I repent of my evil way and have returned to You in full repentance. Help me, O God of my deliverance, so that I may not turn again around fully but walk before You truthfully upright. Hear my prayer. Prolong my life. Let me complete my years in happiness so that I may be enabled to serve You and keep Your statutes with a perfect head.

*From the sickbed confessional prayer*

# Personal Thoughts and Commitments
## for
## Self-Renewal This Week

# Vayigash: Divine Plans

## Genesis 44:18-47:27

**When a person travels a road, let that person make it the road of God, and let him invite God to be his companion.**

*Zohar III, 87b*

- ✔ Finally Joseph reveals his identity to his brothers.
- ✔ The brothers return to Canaan to bring their father and family down to Egypt.
- ✔ An elderly Jacob and his grown son Joseph are tearfully reunited.

## Sunday

**The land of Egypt is before you.**

*Genesis 46:6*

So many temptations. So much to bring me down. And I want only to live.

# *Monday*

**So now it was not you who sent me here but God.**
*Genesis 45:8*

Joseph would undoubtedly identify with the following line from Isaiah: "For My plans are not your plans . . ." (55:8). Another one of Joseph's remarks to his brothers echoes the same theme: "For while you were planning evil against me, God was planning good" (Genesis 50:20). What we intend to happen and what actually happens are often two entirely separate things. That is the essence of "letting go and letting God"—realizing that there is a plan for us above and beyond what we have devised, and that it's OK.

In recovery, I have learned that, instead of being a dead tragic example, I can be a living power of hope and strength, carrying the message of recovery to others. I have come to believe that God's plans for me are much better than my own.

I know somebody in my fellowship whose new house burned down even before he had a chance to move in. He wondered aloud to his sponsor what the purpose of such a misfortune could possibly be. He was told: "Perhaps so you could let a newcomer whose house has just burned down know that one can get through a situation like this without picking up a drug." That person is still coming to meetings today—and so am I. And we never would have planned it that way. Thank God!

# Tuesday

**Do not seek revenge upon the person who
has abused you.**

*Derech Eretz Zuta 2*

Joseph knows what to do. He says simply "I am your brother Joseph" (Genesis 45:4). Such honesty—after all the games, all the deceptions. No more. I can't stand it anymore. No revenge. Just see me for who I really am. Not a Pharaoh. Just your brother.

# Wednesday

**The one whose face is inflamed with anger
shows that the *Sitra Achra*, the spirit of
evil, burns within him.**

*Zohar IV, 179a*

Joseph tells his brothers, "Do not quarrel along the way" (Genesis 45:24). Seems like such friendly advice—the kind of words offered by parents to young children: Don't fight with one another. Ah, but there is more. The truth will have to be told. Don't beat yourself up. I have forgiven you.

# Thursday

**And now, do not be grieved nor angry with yourselves because you sold me here. God sent me before you to preserve life.**

*Genesis 45:5*

A Yiddish proverb puts it well: "What God has sent, no human can prevent." But if our destiny has already been determined, where does that leave us? Should we just give up and passively accept the Divine decree? Were Joseph's brothers, by selling him into slavery, doing him a well-disguised favor? Time and again, the Torah answers, "No." There is Divine Providence, but there is also individual accountability. The way we respond matters. And there are certain things that we can change.

One of them is ourself. As the traditional High Holiday prayer reminds us, "Prayer, penitence, and righteous acts can avert the severe decree." How can a Divine Plan be so contingent on human change? Perhaps we should give God more credit for being infinitely flexible. Or, perhaps, as one rabbi has explained, the fate intended for us does not happen because, by changing our ways, we become different people.

Our purpose as semispiritual beings is to improve as best we can. Perhaps that is why the journey towards recovery so often leads to a spiritual awakening. We regain our sense of purpose and restake our claim in the land of the living. Accepting that our Higher Power has a sometimes inscrutable plan for us does not exempt us from doing our best to change the things we can. As an anonymous philosopher put it, "We may not be able to change the direction of the wind, but we can adjust the sails."

# Friday

**I am God, the God of your father. Do not be afraid to go down to Egypt, for I will make you into a great nation. I Myself will go down with you to Egypt and I Myself will also bring you back.**

*Genesis 47:3-4*

With every Israel of the soul, there must be an Egypt. A going down in order to fully embrace the going up. The illusion of plenty when there is famine. And God will take you by the hand and lead you. That's a promise.

# *Shabbat*

**God has sent me ahead of you to insure
your survival on earth, and to save your
lives in an extraordinary deliverance.**

*Genesis 45:7*

At Twelve Step meetings we are often reminded that when
one door closes, another one opens. But it sure gets scary in
the hallway. Faith and patience. That's the key. Just reflect on
your own life for a minute. How many of the things we worried about turned out much better than we thought they
would? At painful times, we often can't see beyond the curve
of life's road.

May I always have the clear vision to see the bigger picture.
God has sent me on my way, and I must continue the journey
as best I can. How can I begin to fathom what God has
mapped out beyond the corners of my mind? Who could
have known that Joseph's early dreams would eventually
come true? How could we know that Joseph would emerge
from the pit and save the Jewish people from starving their
bodies and souls? Like Joseph, we know not where our lives
will take us. But we can decide which road to take: bumpy
and full of potholes like a winter-weathered roadway, or
smooth like the sea at rest.

Go where God wants you to go. Look for the signals on the
roadway. Don't stop and look back. Just keep on going.

# Questions for Self-Reflection

1. What will it take for me to stop deceiving others and reveal my true self?

2. After all this time, will I have the courage and strength to finally call my former friend and forget what has transpired between us?

3. Why can't I just face the truth?: I am not always in control.

# Notes to Myself

# Sacred Thoughts for Holy Living

I have known all along what I have intended for you, says God, plans for your welfare, not for disaster, to give you a hopeful future.

*Jeremiah 29:11*

# For Renewal, A Psalm

Adonai sets free the prisoners
Adonai opens the eyes of the blind
Adonai raises up those who are bowed down
Adonai loves the righteous
Adonai protects the stranger.
You uphold the orphan and widow
But the way of the wicked, you make crooked.
Adonai will rule forever
Your God, Zion, for all generations
Hallelujah.

*Psalm 146:7-10*

# A Prayer

May it be Your great pleasure, Adonai our God, to give to each person everything that he needs; and may You supply to each and every person what she requires. Praised are You who hears prayer.

*Babylonian Talmud, Berachot 29b*

# Personal Thoughts and Commitments
## for
## Self-Renewal This Week

# Vayechi: Preparing the Future

## Genesis 47:28-50:26

**The Torah gives life to the one who makes use of its light.**

*Babylonian Talmud, Ketubot*

✔ On his deathbed, Jacob blesses his grand-children Ephraim and Manasseh.

✔ Then he blesses all his children.

✔ Fulfilling a promise, following Jacob's death, Joseph goes up to Canaan to bury his father at Machpelah.

✔ Joseph dies in Egypt.

## Sunday

**Jacob lived.**
*Genesis 47:28*

What an expression to use at the end of one's life. Jacob did not die; he lived. Because of all that he had done, because of the legacy of blessings he left his children. We too live beyond the grave. Prepare for it now by living a good life.

# Monday

**And Israel stretched out his right hand, and laid it upon Ephraim's head, who was the younger, and his left hand upon Manasseh's head, guiding his hands wittingly, for Manasseh was the first-born.**

*Genesis 48:14*

"Repent one day before your death" (Pirkei Avot 2:10) is a classic Jewish admonition on the need for perpetual penitence. Since we do not know the day on which we are going to die, it's a good idea to get to it today.

Jacob's final living act is to bless his sons and grandsons from Joseph, and it is an act of great amends. The boy who felt it necessary to fool his father in order to get the blessing rightfully belonging to his older brother has become the man who understands that there are more than enough blessings in this world to go around. By reversing the natural order and placing his right hand on the head of the younger grandson—then blessing them both simultaneously—he shows the hardwon spiritual wisdom of Israel, the one who has successfully struggled against himself to get closer to God.

Ephraim and Manasseh's reaction is equally exemplary. The older son does not become jealous, nor does the younger become arrogant. Family unity in Genesis—finally! No surprise then, that this act became the basis for the traditional Friday night parental blessing said over children to this very day.

Learning from past mistakes, correcting our behavior, and avoiding envy and egotism are all good ways to ensure a brighter future—no matter what happens. In recovery, the future looks a lot better than it used to. With steps and willingness, friends and faith, we *can* get there from here.

# Tuesday

**Great is repentance for it brings deliverance nearer.**
*Babylonian Talmud, Yoma 86b*

A future is impossible without a return to God. There is no other way to say it. But don't just wait. Go out and do something. Bring deliverance for yourself and in doing so, redemption for the world—one person at a time, one step at a time.

# Wednesday

**No one should depend on a miracle to save him. If a miracle has saved him once, he must not depend on a miracle to rescue him a second time.**
*Zohar I, 111b*

It is a miracle that we have survived the abuse we have thrust upon our bodies. And yet we are alive. Don't forget: It is a miracle. Just don't count on it again. Instead, prepare your life so that you don't have to wait for it to happen.

# *Thursday*

**And when Jacob made an end of charging his children, he gathered up his feet into his bed and died.**
*Genesis 49:33*

The Talmud teaches, "Act while you can: While you have the chance, the means, and the strength" (Shabbat 151b). It is a fallacy to think that we "can always get to it tomorrow." Tomorrow may present an entirely new set of challenges. Or we may, for one reason or another, simply be unable to do tomorrow what we put off doing today. In this week's portion, for example, Jacob dies immediately after blessing his children. What if he had waited?

Although recovery wisdom teaches us not to try to do too much at once, we need to be careful not to misinterpret this as a license to be lax. "Easy does it," means, "Don't try to do everything at once," not "Don't try to do anything."

Especially when it comes to trying something new or confronting a problem, fear may get in the way, and we can easily imprison ourselves in a fort of rationalizations. Stop making so much sense! People only do their best when they are striving to be their best. Too much rest leads to rust. How much more fulfilling could we make today by doing something that we have been putting off?

# *Friday*

**Please do not bury me in Egypt.**
*Genesis 47:29*

Jacob spoke of his own impending death, but too many among us are already buried in Egypt. We need to raise ourselves up out of Egypt now, before it's too late.

# Shabbat

**By you shall Israel invoke blessings.**
*Genesis 48:20*

A rabbi was once challenged to defend the notion that there is a place and purpose for everything in God's creation. "Even for atheism?" he was challenged. "Yes," came the reply. "When we see a poor person suffering, we should not assume that God will help him and we need not do so. Instead, we must act as if God did not exist and help him ourselves." God is One but Israel is many.

We do not live by ourselves, in isolation—no matter how separate we sometimes feel. We live in community, interacting with our neighbors, friends, and family. Often, in recovery, we have to rebuild that network, to muster the strength and support necessary to overcome our addiction. In the past, people were not blessed by what we did. We have to face that harsh truth, no matter how painful. Through Jacob, God shows us we have another chance. Through our acts, now, all Israel can be blessed. It seems like an awesome and somewhat impossible task. But consider it. It requires no scientific knowledge or miracle cures. All God is asking of us is to secure the future by living a good life, by positively influencing all those whom we meet. The world can't be redeemed unless we redeem those whom we meet. The world can't be redeemed unless we redeem ourselves, one individual at a time. Imagine the potential we hold deep within us. If only we would work toward that goal of saving self and, by extension, blessing those around us.

# Questions for Self-Reflection

1. What have I buried in Egypt?

2. How have I blessed those around me?

3. What hopes do I carry with me on my journey?

# Notes to Myself

# Sacred Thoughts for Holy Living

Whoever desires to pollute himself with sin will find all of the gates open before him; and whoever desires to attain the highest purity will find all of the forces of goodness ready to help him.

*Babylonian Talmud, Shabbat 104a*

# For Renewal, A Psalm

Restore our resources, Adonai, like watercourses in the Negev.

They who sow in tears shall reap with songs of joy.

Though he goes along weeping carrying the seed bag he shall come back with songs of joy carrying his sheaves.

*Psalm 126:4-6*

# A Prayer

Unite our hearts, O God, to revere Your name. Keep us far from what You hate. Bring us near to what You love. Deal mercifully with us for the sake of Your name.

*Jerusalem Talmud, Berachot 4:2*

# Personal Thoughts and Commitments
## for
## Self-Renewal This Week

# Shemot: Hearing the Call

## Exodus 1:1–6:1

## I will take you out of the misery of Egypt . . . to a land flowing with milk and honey.
### Exodus 3:17

✔ A new Pharaoh arises in Egypt who does not remember the good that Joseph has done and enslaves the Israelite people.

✔ Slavery is brutal and it continues to worsen.

✔ All baby Israelite boys are condemned to death by Pharaoh. One mother, Yocheved, tries to save her son by floating him on the Nile. That child is Moses.

✔ Rescued from the river by the Pharaoh's daughter, Moses is raised as royalty.

✔ After he kills an Egyptian taskmaster, Moses flees to Midian, where he hears God's call from the midst of a burning thornbush.

✔ Joined by his brother Aaron, Moses goes to Pharaoh—but Pharaoh only makes the slavery worse.

## Sunday

**The Israelites were groaning under the bondage and cried out . . . and God took note of them.**
### Exodus 2:33

It works both ways. To hear the call, we have to speak out.

# Monday

**Every son that is born you shall cast into the river.**
*Exodus 1:22*

That river is the Nile, and, if you can possibly forgive the atrocious pun, the "river" that I almost drowned in was called Denial.

Denial is one of the most powerful forces of active addiction. It kept us going down the path of madness long after saner minds would have bailed out, because it kept us from hearing God's call, our own inner wisdom, or *any voice of reason, for that matter.* I think one of the main reasons that we addicts, whatever our poison, invested ourselves so heavily into denial was to avoid the terrifying necessity of having to change.

That investment almost bankrupted us, however. Denial eventually collapses under its own weight of rationalizations, distortions, and lies. Even in recovery, denial remains a formidable adversary. People tend to believe the things they want to believe. Without the "reality-checking" provided by honest soul-searching and the feedback of friends and caring family, we can easily conjure up our own brand of false reality.

Today, let us pray for a clear, honest vision of the way things are. Let us leave denial where it belongs—in Egypt.

# Tuesday

**Only a person who is free is capable of sensing the bitterness of slavery.**

*Rabbi Joseph David of Brisk*

Sometimes we don't even know we are slaves. We get used to it. So far from freedom and so long since we've been there, we don't even know what it feels like any longer. When we hear the call beckoning us back to sobriety, to freedom, we start to hear again, see again, and taste again.

# Wednesday

**Prophecy is given only to those who are broken of heart.**

*Zohar I, 212a*

To hear the call, we have to prepare ourselves. Moses is told: "Do not come closer. Remove your sandals from your feet, for the place on which you stand is holy ground" (Exodus 3:4). Each day we are sober, we realize that we are on holy ground, broken as we may feel. To keep clean, to put our lives back in order requires similar preparation. An extra effort. A special awareness.

# *Thursday*

**And God said: "Do not come any closer. Take your shoes off from your feet, for the place where you're standing is holy ground."**

*Exodus 3:5*

One commentator, the Malbim, explains that, as the shoe is to the foot, so the body is merely the outer garment of the human soul. God is saying, "If you wish to understand My ways and behold My Revelation, you must first set aside your bodily barriers—your drives and urges."

It is similar with recovery. Simply staying away from drugs or drinks is not, by itself, recovery, but it is a highly recommended prerequisite for being able to hear the message of recovery. We need to make ourselves more "mentally barefoot," in order to continue. Taking one's shoes off also suggests a commitment to stay. As Rabbi Lawrence Kushner in his book *Honey from the Rock* has asked: "How long must someone look at a burning bush to know whether or not it is being consumed? Certainly longer than most people look at anything. Longer, in other words, than you need to. More than to see it. Or to use it. Long enough to see if it will be for you an entrance."

One of the most important suggestions made to newcomers in recovery is to attend ninety meetings in ninety days . . . because recovery cannot be learned while one is headed for the door. Part of being willing is being willing to stay for awhile. As they say, if after ninety days you decide that the program is not for you, your misery will be fully refunded. As addicts, our natural tendency is to run. A good part of recovery is learning how *not* to run—and how to be serenely still.

# *Friday*

**The more the Pharaoh afflicted them, the more they grew and filled the land.**

*Exodus 1:12*

All of us have a certain resilience, a bounce-back quality to our lives. Sometimes it hides from us, but it is there. Like our ancestors who fought their slavery with determination, our former addictions give us an even greater commitment to sobriety.

# *Shabbat*

**Please Adonai, I have never been a man of worth, either in times past or now that You have spoke to Your servant.**
*Exodus 3:10*

Our first response to recovery is humility: Who am I that I deserve God's special recognition? Bachya ibn Pakuda teaches in his *Duties of the Heart* that "it is a mark of humility to be happy with what we have." Listen carefully for God's call. And respond to it. Get clean. Stay sober. But realize that God has taken an interest in you because you are worth it. And when you know in your heart what it is that God wants you to do, go ahead and do it. Moses is humbled by his experience. Maybe he is even a little afraid. Who wouldn't be? But then he goes out and does what he has to do. And we are here because of it. It usually takes someone else to show us our slavery, to lead us out to freedom. But once we find the way out, we have to be willing to continue the journey. Pharaoh's armies will continue to chase you. And you will have to continue to evade them. Freedom requires us to listen constantly for the call. So does sobriety. There are risks. That's the way life is.

# Questions for Self-Reflection

1. What can I do to better position myself to hear the call? How can I prepare to respond?

2. Do I have the strength to raise myself to the demands of the call?

3. How is God speaking to me in ways that I hadn't previously realized?

# Notes to Myself

# Sacred Thoughts for Holy Living

One of the Sages said, "I am a child of God, and my neighbor is God's child, too. My work is in the town; his is in the field. I rise early to my work and he rises early to his. He boasts not of his work; I will not boast of mine. And if you say that I do great things and he small, I ask, Have we not learned that it doesn't matter whether a person accomplishes much or little if only he fixes his heart on his Parent in heaven?"

*Babylonian Talmud, Berachot 17a*

# For Renewal, A Psalm

When I was untroubled
I thought, "I will never be shaken," for You,
    Adonai, formed me as a mighty mountain.
When You hid Your face, I was terrified.
I called out to You, Adonai.
Adonai, I appealed to You.
What will be gained from my death?
From my descent in the pit.
Can dust praise You?
Can it declare Your faithfulness?
Respond, Adonai.  Be merciful.
Adonai, help me.
You turned my lament into dancing.
You unfastened my sackcloth and girded me with
    joy so that my whole being might endlessly be
    able to sing songs of praise to You.
Adonai, I will praise You forever.

*Psalm 30:7-13*

# A Prayer

Adonai, my God. I do not desire Your paradise. I do not desire the bliss of the afterworld. I only desire You, Yourself.

*Schneur Zalman of Lyady*

# Personal Thoughts and Commitments
## for
## Self-Renewal This Week

# Va'era: Finding God

## Exodus 6:2-9:35

### By this you shall know that I am Adonai.
*Exodus 7:17*

- ✔ God reveals Godself once again to Moses—this time telling him the name YHWH.
- ✔ The Israelites still refuse to listen to Moses.
- ✔ Moses and Aaron go to Pharaoh and demonstrate God's marvels—but to no avail. Pharaoh's heart is hardened.
- ✔ The first six plagues are cast upon Egypt: blood, frogs, lice, insects, pestilence, and inflammation.

## Sunday

### Let My people go so that they may worship me.
*Exodus 8:16*

The Israelites want their freedom to worship God. Freedom demands responsibility. Sobriety is not simply freedom from chemicals: It is a change of attitude. Slavery is behind you. Now make yourself worthy of the gift of redemption. There is no freedom without God.

# *Monday*

**And I will harden Pharaoh's heart, and multiply My signs and My wonders in the land of Egypt. But Pharaoh will not pay heed . . .**

*Exodus 7:3-4*

With a hardened heart, you can't find God. In the slavery of active addiction, we cut ourselves off emotionally. We tried desperately hard to numb our pain, but the pain did not go away. In fact, it increased. So we just grew more numb . . . until nothing felt good because nothing felt.

Our emotional state and our values color our perspective. If our heart has been hardened by too much hard living, we become oblivious to the signs and wonders of God around us. We are too busy running, hiding, and looking for other things.

Someone once said that coincidences are God's way of staying anonymous. How we choose to look at the world is entirely up to us, but it also affects what we become. The difference between, "Good morning, God!" and, "Good God, morning!" is as significant as the difference between Pharaoh and Moses. The one hears God from a burning bush and the other remains blindly obstinate despite an abundance of dramatic miracles.

In the Jewish view, there is no place where God is not. At any time then, through our thoughts and deeds, we are either attuning ourselves more to God and God's will for us, or we are tuning out. Sometimes, finding God is simply a matter of not looking for distractions . . . and of how you look.

# Tuesday

**When Moses' prayer was answered, Pharaoh
changed his mind. That is the way of the wicked:
When in trouble, they cry out to God. When they
have respite, they return to their evil ways.**
*Exodus Rabbah 10:6*

Let Pharaoh's actions be a lesson to you. Keep the dialogue
going between you and God. That way you won't be able to
return to your evil ways. God will talk you out of it.

# Wednesday

**Truth is heavy; therefore few wear it.**
*Midrash Samuel on Avot 4*

By definition, God always stands in the right—even when
wrong. You can tell God so. It's OK to have such chutzpah in
the face of heaven. But sometimes you have to know when to
admit you are wrong. Admit it to yourself and to others—
especially those you love and may have hurt—then go and
tell it to God.

# *Thursday*

**And Adonai said unto Moses, "See, I have put you in God's stead to Pharaoh . . .**
*Exodus 7:1*

As Rabbi Samson Raphael Hirsch put it, "Only in working out some end can you know God." Many of us think that God can only be encountered through prayer and meditation, but Judaism has always advocated a more activist approach, as well. Rabbi Hirsch provides us with the illuminating insight that faith and purpose walk hand-in hand.

Moses may have first encountered God at the burning bush, but it is only in this week's portion, as he actively goes about fulfilling God's plan, that his initial doubts about his qualifications as a leader are quelled. He learns firsthand that, with God's help, all kinds of miracles can happen.

As active addicts, our main purpose in life became the pursuit of our particular addiction, yet it was that very dead-end road that brought us into recovery. In recovery, we regain a sense of purpose: to learn to live life clean. Believing in a God of our understanding and undergoing a spiritual awakening are key parts of the process, but having that sense of purpose is the catalyst. Slowly, our lives start making sense again.

For those in recovery, the basic plan is to make it through the day without resorting to our addiction, to attend meetings, and to work the steps. In time, as our faith deepens and we remain true to our initial purpose, we will enjoy more meaningful lives. More will be revealed.

# *Friday*

**Early in the morning station yourself before Pharaoh.**
*Exodus 9:13*

Get up early and do it. Don't put it off. Be strong. Only you can prevent the enslavement. Tell the dealer, the bartender, "No"—and mean it.

# *Shabbat*

**In order that you may know that there is none
like Me in all the world.**

*Exodus 9:14*

Miracles are hard to come by. And so is freedom—especially from alcohol and drugs, too much food and sex, and compulsive gambling. In your struggle in recovery, once you have discovered God, keep on discovering. Signs of God's presence surround us; we need only go out and look for them. Influenced by alcohol and drugs, we will never be able to see them. Preoccupied with bodily pleasures, there's no time to look. Listen to the sacred text. God is trying to convince us that there is none like our God in all the world. We have been convinced. Now, can we convince you?

Every age has its own kind of afflictions and miracles. Through them all, God remains the Rock, Eternal. Thousands of people now in recovery have had spiritual reawakenings and dramatic life turnabouts. These are not passing fad nor mass coincidence. The great Jewish scholar Nachmanides agrees: "No one can share in the Torah unless he believes that all affairs and events, concerning the masses or the individual, are miracles, attributing nothing to the natural order of the world." The fact that many things in nature occur with remarkable regularity make it miraculous. We are all a part of creation, renewed each day—in order for us to know God.

# Questions for Self-Reflection

1.  Will God reveal Godself to me as God did with Moses?

2.  Where are the places in my life where I can find God?

3.  Has my heart also been hardened?

# Notes to Myself

# Sacred Thoughts for Holy Living

The one who desires to come nearer to God is helped to do so. The one who desires to sanctify oneself has holiness spread over him.

*Zohar IV, 126a*

# For Renewal, A Hymn

By night in bed I sought You whom my soul
    loves.

I sought You but I did not find You.

I will rise now and go about the city, in the streets
    and in the broad ways.

I will seek You whom my soul loves.

I sought You but I did not find You.

Scarcely had I passed from them when I found
    You whom my soul loves.

*Song of Songs 3:1-4*

# A Prayer

King David said to the prophet Gad: I am in deep distress. Let us fall into the hands of Adonai, for great is God's compassion. But let me not fall into the hands of mortals.

*2 Samuel 24:14*

# Personal Thoughts and Commitments
## for
## Self-Renewal This Week

# Bo: Leaving Egypt Behind

## Exodus 10:1-13:16

**And this shall serve you as a sign on your hand and a reminder on your forehead— in order that the teachings of Adonai may be in your mouth—that with a mighty hand Adonai freed you from Egypt.**

*Exodus 13:9*

✔ Four more plagues: hail, thunder, locusts, and darkness. And then the death of the Egyptian firstborn.

✔ God's signs are displayed, and Pharaoh's heart continues to be hardened.

✔ The Israelites ask to go out and celebrate Passover, and they are delivered from Egypt.

## Sunday

**And there shall be a loud cry in all the land of Egypt, such as has never been or will be heard again.**

*Exodus 11:6*

Don't be afraid to cry for help. You can't do it alone. And that's OK. None of us can. And we all must—in one way or another. People are here to take note of your pain . . . and to help.

# *Monday*

## Remember this day in which you came out from Egypt, out of the house of bondage.
### *Exodus 13:3*

He who does not remember the last time he succumbed to his disease probably hasn't succumbed for the last time. That's one of the main purposes of Twelve Step meetings: "to keep it green," to recall, from the words of a speaker or the sharing of a newcomer, how bad it got "out there." It is a message we need to keep hearing as often as possible, because our disease wants us to forget.

Remembering that we were slaves in Egypt is central to the Jewish perspective. "In each generation, every individual must regard oneself as if personally delivered from Egypt," the Mishnah tells us (Pesachim 10:5). The redemption from Egypt is mentioned several times daily in Jewish prayers. Why is this? Perhaps to inspire gratitude that we are free and to elicit compassion for those less fortunate; to recall the formative experience of the Jewish people; to reiterate the belief that God helped us then and continues to help us now. Perhaps, most of all, to realize that, without God's help, we can never be free.

Remembering slavery is not too difficult for the addict. We have many bitter memories that do not need to be augmented with horseradish. What are the implications of remembering that we are addicts? We recognize that we can never again use successfully. We admit that we need help, that we cannot cure ourselves. We commit ourselves to helping other addicts as we were helped. And, most of all, we are grateful that we finally can break the shackles of self-enslavement.

Remember, this day, clean, is another day of freedom. And set it upon your heart with a smile.

# Tuesday

*Avadim Hayinu.* **We were slaves to Pharaoh in Egypt. . . .
Had the Holy Blessed One not taken our ancestors out of
Egypt, then our children and our children's children would
still be enslaved. . . . Even if we were all scholars, sages or
elders, and learned in the Torah, it would still be our duty
to tell the story of our Exodus from Egypt.**

*Haggadah*

The denial is over. We have a story to tell. Addiction is a
problem we face. There is no shame in it. Now that we have
admitted it, let's overcome it together. And continue to tell
our story.

# Wednesday

**Rabbi Simcha Bunim once observed someone pacing back
and forth, back and forth. "Pardon me," he said to the
man, "but I am anxious about something. I understand why
you went from here to there. I can also understand why
you returned, because on arriving there you realized things
were better here. What I cannot understand is why you
went back there again."**

Egypt may look better through the lens of our addiction.
Short and simple: Don't go back.

# Thursday

**This month shall be to you the beginning of months . . .**
*Exodus 12:2*

Not only is the difference between freedom and slavery profound enough to be celebrated as a new beginning, but now time itself is perceived differently. In recovery, each day is a new blessing.

The Kotzker Rebbe observed that there was something even worse for the Israelites than the hardships of slavery: "They were willing to bear the Egyptian yoke, and it was from these 'bearings' that they first had to be delivered." There is a major difference, spiritually, between the slave who wants to be free and the slave who has grown comfortable in slavery. One can become comfortable with addiction, too. It is only when the misery of the disease exceeds the misery of withdrawing from it, that we become willing to do something about it. We may try repeatedly to quit by ourselves. We may seek psychiatric help. Or we may join a Twelve Step program. But the key thing is that we no longer want to be slaves.

Once we come to that point, we can't go back again. We will continue to have thoughts and urges about using from time to time. Old habits die hard, but they will never again be as much fun as in the beginning. Because slipping unintentionally into slavery is one thing, but willingly going back into slavery is quite another. Remembering that we chose to leave behind the slavery of active addiction because it became unbearable can help us stay away. We don't ever have to go back.

# Friday

**We will go with our young and old.**
*Exodus 10:9*

Everyone left Egypt, which means that each and every one of us was there. Kids and adults drink and do drugs. Food, sex, and gambling have no age requirements. Don't forget it. Open your eyes and see what we have done before it is too late. Let's go out and rescue one another. We don't want to go down to Egypt ever again.

# Shabbat

## And thick darkness descended all the land of Egypt.
### *Exodus 10:22*

And the people of Egypt were thrown into deep despair. Perhaps it was a means to get the Egyptians to identify with the bleak perspective of the slaves. That tired, almost subhuman feeling that nothing matters, nothing changes, and no one cares. How often have we felt this way? Without light, nothing can be seen. But our sages tell us that this was no ordinary darkness that plagued the Egyptians. The commentator Sforno described it thus: "Generally, darkness is really the absence of light and can be dispelled by lighting a fire. But this darkness that was so thick, it could be touched. It was a darkness of a deeper nature." Boy, do we know what he's talking about. Gloom. Despondency. Disillusionment. We have felt all of these feelings and more in our addiction. There seemed to be no way to find the light. The Gerer Rebbe teaches that this kind of darkness is so dense that people can't see one another in it. And that is the worst of all. Why? When people "see" their neighbors, when they "see" their neighbors' distress, they can reach out to help them. Shabbat casts its light on the world. It is a special kind of light that is a reflection of the world beyond. In this light, we are able to see others—our family and friends—and everything around us. No longer do we look through the lens of our addiction; in its stead, we see everything through the light of redemption.

# *Questions for Self-Reflection*

1. How can I remove the darkness from my life?

2. What are those plagues from which I still need to be delivered?

3. How should I celebrate my redemption?

# *Notes to Myself*

# Sacred Thoughts for Holy Living

The Sages tell us that there were Jews whose hearts and souls became so enslaved that they did not want to be set free. When Moses brought them the good news of God's intention to liberate them, they said to him: "God decreed that we must be slaves for four hundred years, and our time is not up."

*Exodus Rabbah 15:1*

# For Renewal, A Psalm

When Israel came forth out of Egypt

The house of Jacob from a people of strange
    language

Judah became Your sanctuary

Israel Your dominion.

The sea saw it and fled

The Jordan turned backward

The mountains skipped like rams,

The hills like young sheep.

*Psalm 114:1-4*

# A Prayer

Daily You renew our souls, restoring us as You redeemed our ancient nation Israel from slavery to freedom, from sorrow to triumph, blessing our people with the springtime of its life, to be renewed by all of us each year. Healer of our wounds, holy God, do not abandon us to enemies without and within.

*Adapted from* Siddur Sim Shalom
*by Rabbi Jules Harlow*

Published by The Rabbinical Assembly and the United Synagogue of America, © 1985, by the Rabbinical Assembly. Reprinted by permission.

# Personal Thoughts and Commitments
## for
## Self-Renewal This Week

# Beshallach: At the Crossroads

*Exodus 13:17-17:16*

**Whether you turn to the right or to the left,
your ears will hear these words behind you:
"This is the way, follow it."**

*Isaiah 30:21*

✔ In a route chosen by God, not by Moses, the people take the long road to Canaan and are stopped at the Red Sea—even as the Egyptian armies are in pursuit.

✔ Miraculously, they cross the river on dry land, and their pursuers are drowned.

✔ Miriam leads the people in dance on the other shore. Then they set out on their long journey.

## Sunday

**The people may have a change of heart when they see
war and return to Egypt.**

*Exodus 13:17*

When things get rough, our tendency is to return to the more familiar—even though we longed to leave when we were there. Break the mold. Battle the enemy of addiction whenever it confronts you. Don't go back to Egypt. There you were a slave. Now you can be free.

# *Monday*

## And the Israelites went into the midst of the sea on dry ground . . .
### *Exodus 14:22*

Very often, we manage to paralyze ourselves into indecision. We analyze, we rationalize, we procrastinate. We talk it into the ground. And yet we do not act.

According to the Midrash (Exodus Rabbah 21:9), God did not split the Red Sea until the children of Israel walked in up to their necks. Even when it comes to miracles, God wants us to get as far as we can by ourselves. Do not rely on miracles to bolster your faith. More often than not, the road to every-day miracles is paved with strong faith and the best that we can do.

It's the same in recovery. Walking into a room full of strange people for the first time and admitting that you're an addict is not easy. Opening yourself up to other people is not easy. Facing life on life's terms is not easy. But we have learned that the alternative is worse. Faced with the choice of Pharaoh's army in hot pursuit and a vast sea and a promise from God, it is better to get wet.

Life is like that, too; we sometimes have to get uncomfortable in order to get comfortable. If we keep doing the things we've always done, we're just going to get the results we've always gotten. Many people effectively excuse themselves from life. They are too old for this. Too heavy. Too scared. Fear of failing and fear of trying new things and fear of being seen as less than perfect are all forms of self-enslavement, too. In recovery, we learn new patterns, meet new people, and do new things. And, quite often, it's a whole lot of fun.

We will go further than our wildest dreams if we just do the best we can and have faith that our Higher Power is there to help. But first we have to get wet.

# Tuesday

**Where there is life, there is hope.**
*Jerusalem Talmud, Berachot 9:1*

Sometimes when we are at the crossroads and have to make a vital decision, we do not know which way to turn, what to do, where to go. We muster all the personal strength from the very limits of our being. Then, and only then, do we ask God for Divine inspiration. And watch the miracle work inside of us.

# Wednesday

**If you walk straight, you will not stumble.**
*Yiddish saying*

What else is there to say? Stay clean, and you will be able to see clearly where you are going. But if you do stumble, pick yourself right up and keep on going.

# *Thursday*

**For it were better for us to serve the Egyptians, than that
we should die in the wilderness.**
*Exodus 14:12*

**Then sang Moses and the children of Israel . . .**
*Exodus 15:1*

**Would that we had died by the hand of the Lord in Egypt...
[instead of dying from hunger here in the wilderness]**
*Exodus 16:3*

Talk about mercurial emotions! It doesn't take very long for
the children of Israel to go from *kvetching* to singing God's
praises . . . and back to *kvetching* again.

When we are in the midst of major change, many powerful
feelings come to the surface, and they are often as fast as they
are fleeting. Adrenalin, the body's own excitement drug,
pumps through our veins, practically screaming at us to do
*something*. But the thing that *feels* right at this very moment
may not always be the right thing.

Some changes take longer than others. The children of Israel
have witnessed some of the most spectacular miracles ever,
yet they are reluctant to turn their lives over to the care of
God. The sure comforts of slavery—regular meals and familiar surroundings—seem preferable to the strange new
uncertainties of the present. In short, they are still thinking
like slaves.

A suggestion commonly made to Twelve Step newcomers is
not to make any major changes in the first year. It takes time
for the fog to lift. Not every feeling has to be acted upon. It is
better to share our feelings, seek the more dispassionate guidance of friends and therapists, and let the healing process
take deeper root.

# *Friday*

**Say to the Israelite community, "Advance toward Adonai,
for God has heard your grumbling."**
*Exodus 16:9*

That's always the direction to go in—from wherever you
stand. Walk toward the light. It will illumine your heart.

# Shabbat

**Then Miriam the prophet, Aaron's sister, took a timbrel in her hand, and all the women went out after her in dance.**
*Exodus 15:20*

There are times when you can stop along your journey and rest. No more decisions to make. No need to worry about which way to go. Just being there is enough. You are alive. Be thankful for it. But rejoice—as Miriam and the women of Israel did after our ancestors crossed the Red Sea. The Red Sea presented their passageway from slavery to freedom. Once the waters joined themselves together again and the Egyptians perished (remember and be mindful of it), we knew we were finally on our way home. There were no plans, no rehearsals. They just got up and danced and danced and danced.

The dance was more than just celebration. It helped prepare them for the journey that followed. Being free is only the beginning. We have to go beyond the chemicals, beyond the sex, beyond the food. The dance of Miriam and her sisters, the whoops of joy and laughter that seem integral to recovery at work share a common bond. They are the spontaneous expressions of survivors. There is an indescribably profound sense of exhilaration just to have survived against the odds: a sense of having been delivered. Redeemed. And infinitely blessed. Every Jew who walked across the Red Sea that day and every person who walks into a Twelve Step meeting and decides to stay experiences the miracle of redemption.

In the nurturing womb of Shabbat, ask yourself the hard question: What got us there in the first place? Face the facts, because that stuff will always be there. We have to make sure that there is no room for it. Fill yourself with Shabbat, and nothing else will be able to get even close.

# Questions for Self-Reflection

1. Am I prepared to take the first step into the raging waters, the first step toward redemption?

2. Who continues to pursue me—and why can't I move forward?

3. Why am I reticent to dance?

## Notes to Myself

# Sacred Thoughts for Holy Living

The Rabbi of Rizhyn tells of a young man who came to him. His complaint: "During the hours when I devote myself to my studies, I feel life and light. However, the feeling is gone the moment I stop studying. What shall I do?" The Rabbi of Rizhyn told him: "That is just like a person who makes his way through the forest on a dark night. For a while, another person joins him with a lantern. But when they part from one another at the crossroads, the first person must grope through the dark on his own. If one carries his own light with him, he never has to be afraid of the darkness."

# For Recovery, A Psalm

Adonai, my heart is not haughty nor my eyes
    lofty

Neither do I exercise myself in things too great
    or in things too wonderful for me.

Surely, I have stifled and quieted my soul

Like a weaned child with its mother

My soul is with me like a weaned child.

O Israel, hope in Adonai

From this time forth and forever.

*Psalm 131:1-3*

# A Prayer

Adonai, I have heard stories about You and I am awed by Your deeds. Adonai, review Your work in the midst of the years. Make them known. Although You [are right to be angry] remember [and show] compassion [to me].

*Habakkuk 3:2*

# Personal Thoughts and Commitments
## for
## Self-Renewal This Week

# Yitro: Sinai

## Exodus 18:1-20:23

**There are occasions in our life when we can grasp the manner of our existence in a single moment.**

*Babylonian Talmud, Avodah Zarah 10b*

✔ The Israelites have finally arrived at Sinai. They camp at the foot of the mountain—and wait.

✔ Moses goes up the mountain. God reveals Torah to the people through Moses.

✔ The Ten Commandments are given to the people, one at a time.

## Sunday

**Go to the people and warn them to stay pure today and tomorrow.**
*Exodus 19:10*

Revelation continues. It is more than a one-time event. It is constant. Stay clean—so that you are always ready for it, always in the state of Sinai.

# *Monday*

## I stood between Adonai and you.
*Deuteronomy 5:5*

The "I" in this verse refers to Moses, who is recalling the events at Sinai. The Jewish tradition holds that we were all present at Sinai (one midrash imaginatively describes how all the women's bellies turned to glass, so all the unborn generations in them could witness the event!). While the Rabbi of Kobrin also puts all of us in the line—or, more accurately, on the line—he has a different understanding of these words.

He says that the "I" is the perennial barrier that stands between God and us. He who offers up his "I," on the other hand, leaves nothing between him and his Creator. It is to him that this verse applies: "I am my beloved's, and his desire is toward me." When my "I" has become my beloved's (God's), and my desire is God, then does God turn toward me in love.

Addiction is very much an "I" disease. That's why belief in a Higher Power is such a critical step towards getting better. Faith gives us a healthier perspective; it gets us off our self-obsessed, grandiose, dreadfully lonely mountaintops. By looking heavenward, we can bring ourselves back to earth.

"I have to get out of my way" is a sentiment often shared in the meeting rooms. It means that our "hyper-thinking" often outsmarts us, our wanting often dissatisfies us, and our resistance to change often hurts us.

Recovery is a "we" program. Perhaps the best way to treat the "I" disease is with "I-drops." As the "I" drops in importance, the better we'll be.

# Tuesday

**One who is too full of himself has no room for
the Holy One.**

*Menachem Mendl of Kotzk*

Think about it. If a container is filled up, nothing else can be put in. But if you empty it halfway—especially of nonessential ingredients and air—there's plenty of room. Now what are you going to do?

# Wednesday

**The voice of humans is calculated to be heard;
but that of God to be really and truly seen. Why?
Because all that God says are not words, but
actions which the eyes perceive and the ears do.**

*Philo of Alexandria*

What you hear at Sinai, you see in the world around you. No need to wait at the foot of the mountain. Just go outside and open your eyes—and you will hear the words.

# *Thursday*

**Moses brought forth the people out of the camp to meet God: They stood at the other side of the mount.**
*Exodus 19:17*

The Revelation at Sinai is celebrated during the festival of Shavuot, also known as "the time of the giving of our Torah." Why isn't it called "the time of the receiving of our Torah?" Rabbi Meir Alter of Ger taught that the giving happened at one specified time, but the receiving of the Torah happens at every time and in every generation. It happens every time we study, every time we do a mitzvah. Rashi puts it slightly differently: "Torah must be totally new to you each day."

Recovery, too, must be kept continually fresh. It is not a one-shot, quick-fix deal, but something that, if it is to work, must keep happening—a "daily maintenance program," as some have said. The most inspiring stories and messages that we hear fade away all too soon, because our disease wants us to forget, to despair, and to relapse. Recovery is a lifelong process of arresting the disease of addiction, one day at a time. We get better, but we don't get cured.

Torah, too, never ends. The Revelation of the Torah may have begun at Sinai, but if it does not continue within us, it becomes mere history or myth. A fossilized spirituality is like no spirituality at all. Recovery is freely available, but only if it is willingly received. It is very much to our spiritual advantage to stay open to both recovery and Torah.

# *Friday*

**Do not commit adultery.**
*Exodus 20:13*

Sacred trust is the foundation of all relationships. We live all of our lives in relationships. These relationships are built on a sense of mutuality, of give and take. Relationships falter when the taking, taking, taking outweighs the giving.

# Shabbat

**Do not covet . . . anything that is your neighbor's.**
*Exodus 20:14*

Actually, the Bible offers a list for beginners. Those of us who have had years of experience in coveting as adults know that there are many things that should have been included in the list that are easy targets of obsession. Maybe the Bible's authors just didn't dream of these at the time. Or maybe they just wanted to get you started, figuring you could fill in the empty spaces on your own.

Like so many other things in life, coveting has a good, productive side as well as a dark, evil, destructive one. That delicate balance is part of the rich, green landscape of our lives, adding fire and contentment, at the same time, to the often routine patterns of everyday living.

The "journey for the tenth" as I call it, has a different road map for different people, but sooner or later, the destination is the same for all. We eventually think to ourselves, "Wow, I wish I could have that!" To want something is not an evil thing. It is a natural human drive, intricately tied to our existence in this world of things. We all have the urge to own things, especially those items which we think will make our lives easier, more enjoyable, and, especially, raise our standard of living in the face of our neighbors.

Dreams can be comforting. To fantasize is healthy. But to covet, to be overwhelmed by an almost insatiable urge to possess, is contrary to Jewish common sense, to everyday Jewish sechel. At the core of coveting seems to be a dissatisfaction with our own life. This is what makes it wrong. Material goods, however terrific they make us feel, do not have the necessary ingredient to call up a transforming experience. Like drugs and alcohol, luxury items may make us feel good; but the effects of both are temporary and illusory. The reverse is true of a spiritual life where the effects are real—and lasting.

# Questions for Self-Reflection

1. What am I waiting for?

2. What can I do to make sure that I hear God speak to me more clearly?

3. How can I purify myself so that I truly become a vessel for God to speak in this world?

# Notes to Myself

# Sacred Thoughts for Holy Living

In one's approach to God there is no straight way of going up. It is always ascent and descent and ascent. Hence, authentic repentance—"down" and then "up"—is greater than constant piety.

*Hasidic teaching*

# For Renewal, A Psalm

Listen, Adonai is on the waters . . .

Hark! Adonai is powerful.

Hark! Adonai is full of majesty.

Hark! Adonai shakes the wilderness . . .

And in Your temple, everyone just says "Glory!"

*Psalm 21:3-4, 8-9*

# A Prayer

Cause me to return, Avinu, to Your Torah. Draw me near, Malkeinu, to Your service. And bring me back in complete repentance. Praised are You, Adonai, who delights in repentance.

*Adapted from the fifth benediction*
*in the "Shemoneh Esreh"*
*for the morning service*

# Personal Thoughts and Commitments
## for
## Self-Renewal This Week

# Mishpatim: Rules to Live By

## Exodus 21:1–24:18

**For the very beginning of wisdom is the desire of discipline, and the care of discipline is love.**
*Song of Songs Rabbah 6:17*

✔ The laws that distinguish Israel are given: laws on worship, slavery/servants, and injuries.

✔ Additional laws on property and proper behavior which have moral impact are articulated.

✔ As an affirmation of the covenant, specific rules for the Temple cult are listed.

## Sunday

**These are the rules that you shall set before them.**
*Exodus 21:1*

A holy life demands rules. No way to get around it—nor would we want to. These are the rules to live by, that make us better people, getting better at it every day.

# Monday

## Keep yourselves far from a false matter . . .
*Exodus 23:7*

This Torah text specifically refers to spurious legal cases, but it also has obvious wider applications as a general rule of life. Associating with liars, bending the truth a bit whenever it's convenient, even tolerating the dishonesty of others all compromise us morally.

We become compromised because little lies lead to larger ones, just as surely as doing whatever we wanted to do led us to places where we never wanted to be. In recovery, we learn that certain guidelines help promote the self-control and attitudes that make clean living possible. Sometime we may feel restricted by these "suggestions." Many times, we reluctantly drag ourselves to a meeting when we'd much rather be someplace else. Yet we have come to understand that these restrictions are for our own benefit.

The rules of Torah living can often seem stifling, too. Indeed, a common Talmudic term for them is "the yoke of heaven." And yet, they can lead to much joy. The many proscribed activities on the Sabbath may seem severely limiting at first, but, in practice, Shabbat is the most liberating day of the week.

In the quest for spiritual growth, what seems restrictive at first actually opens us up a bit more spiritually. The discomfort of learning new ways will pass (and return . . . and pass again), but it is short-term pain for long-term gain—the exact opposite of addictive behavior!

As the Talmud puts it, "Israel is shielded by its precepts as a dove by its wings" (Shabbat 130a). Living clean will take us higher.

# Tuesday

**Greater is one who prompts a person to do
good than the one who does it.**
*Babylonian Talmud, Baba Batra 9a*

Reach out. The person who comes into a meeting or to prayer may feel uncomfortable, strange. You were there once. Somebody reached out to you. Now is the time to repay that debt. And keep on repaying it.

# Wednesday

**Ascend a step and choose a friend.**
*Babylonian Talmud, Yebamot*

The addict is not alone. He has family, friends, survivors to call on. Don't forget. They need us, too. And we need them.

# *Thursday*

## Adonai said to Moses, "Come up to Me . . ."
### *Exodus 24:12*

God is always saying "Come up to Me," and Judaism teaches that our souls are forever yearning to get closer to God. But we keep getting in our way, and that's what the *mitzvot* are really for. As Abraham ibn Ezra wrote in his *Yesod Morah*, "The essence of all precepts is to make the heart upright." In other words, to keep us spiritually straight.

The Talmud tells us that 613 precepts were given to Moses: the 365 negative ("thou shalt not") commandments corresponding to the days of the year and the 248 positive ones corresponding to the number of joints in the human body (Makkot 23b). In other words, by fulfilling the commandments to the best of his or her ability, a Jew serves God with all his or her body, all the time.

Any admitted addict or alcoholic knows all too well the limitations of "living life my way." The Twelve Steps are a program that makes it possible to stay clean, grow spiritually, and enjoy life more. They are not rules, but principles that are possible to practice on a daily basis. Torah commandments, too, are spiritual vessels. Done right, with feeling as important as form, they light us within, sensitize us to the holy, and help us step more surely before God. As the Talmud says, "The whole Torah exists only for the sake of peace" (Gittin 59b). Peace among nations. Peace between neighbors. And peace within ourselves.

# *Friday*

## When you see the ass of your enemy lying under its burden and would refrain from raising it, you shall nevertheless raise it with him.
### *Exodus 23:5*

Get out of yourself. Don't let distant pain stand in the way of your present growth. If someone needs help, go out and help him. Don't worry if it's a neighbor or a friend or someone who did you dirty. All are God's creations.

# Shabbat

**You shall be holy to me.**
*Exodus 22:30*

Being holy means being in a different kind of space. Special. Consecrated. Separate. But we don't get there just because God says it. Or even because we say it. We get there because we want to be there. And God *wants* us to be there. Believe it. The Talmud says it best, "God helps those who come to purify themselves" (Avodah Zarah 55a). We have walked away from all the chemicals. We have set before ourselves a new code of discipline for living free from addiction. We have raised ourselves up with God as our foundation and support. In doing so, we are closer to God. But in order to be really alive in this newly found life, we have to be prepared to set limits and live by rules. To know what we really can do— now that we are clean—we have to search out the holy in the world, to raise ourselves beyond the beckoning profanity that threatens to bring us down.

Don't confuse being holy with being spiritual. That's as false a notion as true lovers who do not quarrel. Holiness is a kind of spiritual intimacy, a commitment to letting God into your life—which thereby encourages you to act accordingly. It is where faith moves us. We advance from believing in a Higher Power toward a desire to do the holy work of that Higher Power. The more *mitzvot* we do, the holier we are: in deed! Some people just entering recovery have little notion of the sense of joy that awaits them. So too it is with holiness. We experience a level of ecstasy just beyond the border of human understanding.

Listen to the words of God: "You shall be holy." Work at it. Live your life by it. And believe it. "You shall be holy."

# Questions for Self-Reflection

1. What attempts have I made to establish a code of discipline for myself, one that will raise me closer to God?

2. How has the way I live my life affirmed my partnership in the covenant?

3. Which areas of my life require more discipline?

# Notes to Myself

# Sacred Thoughts for Holy Living

It is not your obligation to complete the work, but neither are you free from doing all you can.

*Pirkei Avot 2:21*

# For Renewal, A Psalm

Teach me, Adonai, the way of Your statutes

And I will keep it at every step.

Give me understanding so that I keep Your law

And serve it with a whole head.

Make me walk in the path of Your command-
    ments for I delight in them.

*Psalm 119:33-35*

# A Prayer

Rabbi Chiya: May it be Your will, Adonai our God, that our Torah may be our occupation, and that our heart may not be sick nor our eyes darkened.

*Babylonian Talmud, Berachot 16b*

# Personal Thoughts and Commitments
## for
## Self-Renewal This Week

# *Terumah:*
# *Sanctuary and Service*

## *Exodus 25:1-27:19*

**Like a swift moving fire which does not cease or rest until it has accomplished its purpose, so must one's energy be in the service of God.**

*Moshe Chaim Luzatto*, Mesillat Yesharim

- ✔ God gives Moses further instructions concerning the building of the Tabernacle.
- ✔ At its center will be the Ark, to house the Ten Commandments.
- ✔ The lamp stand and tent are also described, but it is hard to visualize them.
- ✔ And the altar—which will eventually serve as the model for the Temple altar—is also built.

## *Sunday*

**Note well and follow the pattern for them that are being shown you on the mountain.**

*Exodus 25:40*

God shows you what you need to do until you are ready to discover it on your own. Pay attention. The details are important. Especially if you want to stay clean—and live.

# Monday

**And you shall overlay it with pure gold, within
and without shall you overlay it.**
*Exodus 25:11*

Even on the inside, where no one could see it, the Ark was lined with the finest gold—to teach us, according to Rabbi Joseph Hertz, "that man must be as pure in mind and heart as he appears pure in outward manner and bearing."

Social acceptability is not the same as recovery. Indeed, it may well have been one of our cleverest forms of denial. As long as we got good grades, or functioned adequately at our jobs, or just got increasingly ingenious and sneaky about concealing our addiction, we could not possibly have a problem. Meanwhile, inside, we knew what we were doing, and it made us feel rotten. It was only a matter of time before our elaborate facade crumbled like a house of cards. There was such an extreme contrast between our outer appearance and our inner reality. No wonder we were so unbalanced!

Integrity and balance are indispensable spiritual principles. When our actions are consistent with our feelings, beliefs, and values, we are in harmony with ourselves. We need "to walk it like we talk it," or else we lose the beat. Recovery is an "inside job."

Today, we can be grateful for living less compulsively. We can examine our actions, consider our feelings, and work toward reconciling any conflict in a healthier way.

# Tuesday

**One should not choose the form in which he wishes to perform the services of Adonai, but he should perform it in any manner the opportunity affords. He should be like a vessel into which anything may be poured.**

*The Apter Rav*

The Twelfth Step says it, too. You can recite it by memory: "Having had a spiritual awakening as a result of these Steps, we tried to carry this message to alcoholics, and to practice these principles in all our affairs." But service is more than words. Carry the message. Do it on the streets—but in the synagogue, too!

# Wednesday

**Three things destroy worship: First, contempt for anyone; second, lack of faith; and third, an unclean life.**

*Rabbi Nachman of Bratzlav*

That's all there is to it. If you want to reach God through prayer, clean up your act. Let go of the negative energy. Start by saying, "*Ani maamin:* I believe with perfect faith. . . ."

# Thursday

**And let them make Me a Sanctuary, that I may
dwell among them.**
*Exodus 25:8*

Since the text is referring to the Sanctuary, shouldn't it more
properly read, "that I may dwell within it?" No, one commentator explains. We are instructed here that each child of
Israel should make space for the Holy Presence within his or
her own heart. If all the Jews build such a tabernacle, God
will then dwell within each heart.

God wants the heart (Sanhedrin 106b). God wants us to
serve not out of fear nor even out of obligation, but out of
desire. And what is the service of the heart? It is prayer.
When we want to pray to God, when we pray with all our
heart, our soul finds sanctuary within God and vice versa.
Rabbi Nachman of Bratzlav well knew the connection
between heart and prayer: "A person should pray with such
devotion that his heart is as if it were poured out like water
before *Adonai" (Likkutei Etzot Ha'shalem)*.

During active addiction, we tried to find a place, within our
heads, where everything felt good and problems could at least
temporarily disappear. But those hiding places were built on
shaky ground. More and more yielded less and less. Many
were the times we prayed, "Please God, let me survive this,
and I'll never start again." But, alas, even our prayers, though
born of honest desperation, were distorted. We could not
keep our word.

Today we can. Through prayer and meditation we can find
peace of mind and the guidance we need. We can let God in.
We can face life's challenges with clarity and faith.

# Friday

**Tell the Israelite people to bring me gifts; you shall accept
gifts from every person whose heart moves him.**
*Exodus 25:2*

God does not need gifts. God does not need anything. But we
do. The gifts are God's way of allowing us to connect.
Anything is acceptable.

# Shabbat

**There I will meet you.**
*Exodus 25:22*

A holy place for holy business. It's not some distant space, near some distant mountain. Nor is it a magnificent building, well-appointed with crystal and gold. No nature walks or desert wanderings are necessary to find the perfect spot. The meeting place is buried deep inside of you. Dig it out. Unearth it. Let it surface. One commentator, the Malbim, wrote that each person has to build a tabernacle for God in his heart in order for God to dwell there. But there has got to be room. If your heart is filled with anger and bitterness, there may be no building space left. We understand. The pain still makes you crazy. And the memories clog your emotions. But it has got to stop. Such negative energy cannot sustain your soul. Only you can—that is, you and God. But God's got to be there. And you have to let God in.

Our people carried the Tabernacle wherever they went. It was their statement of faith. They were not afraid or embarrassed to show others that they believed deeply in God. And neither are we. So carry your Tabernacle and hold your head up high. *Shiru Ladonai.* Sing songs of praise to God. And open your heart to God and to others—who are made in God's image. Don't worry. There's plenty of room.

# Questions for Self-Reflection

1. What have I placed at the center of my life?

2. Where is the altar in my life?

3. What should I do to serve God?

## Notes to Myself

# Sacred Thoughts for Holy Living

Our Sages tell us that we should only be concerned with today. The same applies to serving God. You should only think of today, the present hour. When a person wants to begin serving God, it seems like too heavy a burden to bear. But if you think that you only have today, it will not be a burden at all. Don't put things off and say, "I'll start tomorrow, tomorrow I will pray with strength and devotion," etc. The human world consists of nothing except the day and the hour that we stand in now. Tomorrow is a completely different world.

*Rabbi Nachman of Bratzlav*

# For Renewal, A Psalm

My Master, open my lips
And my mouth will declare your praise.
For you do not want sacrifice,
Otherwise I would give it;
A burnt offering You do not desire.
The correct offering to God
Is a broken spirit,
A broken and humbled heart.

*Psalm 51:17-19*

# A Prayer

How lovely are your tents, O Jacob, your dwelling places O Israel. In your abundant loving acts of kindness, O God, let me enter Your house, reverently to worship in your holy temple.

Adonai, I love Your house, the place where Your presence dwells.

So I would worship with humility; I would seek blessing in the presence of God, my Maker.

May my prayer now, Adonai, find favor before You.

In your great love, O God, answer me with your saving truth.

*"Mah Tovu," from the morning service*

# Personal Thoughts and Commitments
## for
## Self-Renewal This Week

# Tetzaveh: Holy Instructions

## Exodus 27:20-30:10

**Wash yourself, make yourself clean, put away
the evils of your doings.**

*Isaiah 1:16*

✔ God offers instructions for kindling the eternal
light, to be a constant reminder of God's presence in our midst.

✔ The priestly garments, especially those of the
High Priests and described in great detail,
including the mysterious *Urim* and *Thummim*.

## Sunday

**You shall instruct all who are skillful whom I
have endowed with skill.**

*Exodus 28:3*

When you want to get the job done, don't do it all by yourself. God could have built the Tabernacle. That would have
been easy compared to mountains. Everyone has his or her
own strength, a talent of which to be proud, including you.
But don't think you got there on your own. God helped you
along the way—and continues to do so.

# *Monday*

**And Aaron shall burn thereon incense of sweet spices . . .**

*Exodus 30:7*

As the sweet smell of incense rises skyward and lifts the spirit, so does prayer, which has replaced the Temple rites. As it says in Psalm 141:2: "Let my prayer be prepared as incense before you."

The Rabbis explained that each of the four letters of the Hebrew word for incense—*ketoret*—stood for an important spiritual quality. The "k" for *kedushah*, holiness; the "t" for *taharah*, purity; the "r" for *rachamim*, compassion; and the "t" for *tikvah*, hope.

All of these qualities play an important role in our recovery. Any time we pray, or think about God's will for us, or study Torah, or do anything that brings us closer to God, we are engaged in holy activity. Staying clean is the "purity" that makes continued recovery possible. Reaching out to help others in the fellowship, especially newcomers, is the essence of compassion. And hope that it will get better is what gets us through the day . . . and keeps us coming back.

Smell is the most spiritual of senses. An aroma is, after all, invisible. May the words of our prayers curl up towards heaven in sweet wisps of sincerity and gratitude.

# Tuesday

**The Divine test of a person's worth is not theology but life.**
*Babylonian Talmud, Baba Kamma 38a*

How do you respond to holy instructions? That's all there is to it. You do what you have to do—and stop talking so much about it. Let your life be a model, and not your words.

# Wednesday

**Words of Torah need each other. What one passage locks up, the other unlocks.**
*Numbers Rabbah 19:27*

Ah! The key to understanding. Listen. Learn. Keep listening. Keep learning. Then study some more.

# *Thursday*

**And Aaron and his sons you shall bring to the door of
the tent of meeting and shall wash them with water.**
*Exodus 29:4*

"Who may ascend the mountain of God?" the Psalmist asks
(24:4). "One with clean hands and a pure heart." Israel's
priests are to be completely washed before performing their
atoning rituals on behalf of Israel. The moral symbolism is
clear: To come closer to God, both our outsides and insides
need to be cleansed.

Teshuvah, repentance, can occur any time one is ready to so
wash. A line in the Yom Kippur "Amidah" prayer reads, "I
stand before You as a vessel full of shame and confusion."
The Belzer Rebbe comments: "We implore Adonai to wash
away our shame and impurity as easily as one may clean a
dirty vessel."

One of the most noticeable things about people in recovery,
after they have been coming around for awhile, is how much
better they start to look: better groomed, better dressed, eyes
more full of life, smiles instead of tightly buttoned lips. The
ironic truth is, while living the self-obsessive addictive
lifestyle, we usually are too busy to bother taking care of ourselves. But the key to serenity, to recovery, and to spiritual
growth, is to balance outside behavior with inside values—
and to keep both clean on a daily basis. Meetings are the
spiritual equivalent of a morning shower. Warm prayers, too,
thwart our tendency to wallow in ourselves.

# *Friday*

**Aaron shall carry the instrument of decision for the
Israelites over his heart before Adonai at all times.**
*Exodus 28:30*

That is some responsibility. So let's leave it to Aaron. You
don't have to bear the world's burden on your shoulders.
Just stay away from the gambling tables. Don't touch the
bottle. That's your instrument of decision.

# Shabbat

**It shall be a law for all time for you and
your offspring to come.**
*Exodus 28:40*

Call this statement unconditional. This is not feel-good
Judaism. Torah is eternal. And commitment is forever. Half-
hearted allegiance of any kind falls short. The words of
Torah may be rich and resonant, but its poetry is more than
just pretty words on unusual parchment. And the Program is
no substitute either. Maybe that's a strong statement, maybe
it's even a heresy, but it has to be said. Judaism and AA will
lead you to sobriety and personal redemption. Neither can
get you to both on your own. Serenity not holiness. You have
to be willing to take the journey and follow the instructions
to get from one to the other. We believe that they can work
together. So do you. One enriches the other. The Twelve Steps
and Torah work well together. Now that that's been said, let's
get down to the business of living, making life better for us
and for those we love. There's only one way to do it. Stay off
the chemicals and away from the addicted behaviors; lead a
life inspired by the teachings of Torah. Begin small, one mitzvah at a time.

# Questions for Self-Reflection

1. What do I do to remind myself of God's constant presence in my life?

2. How have I lived a holy life and inspired others to do so?

# Notes to Myself

# Sacred Thoughts for Holy Living

Run after doing the smallest good deed and flee from transgression, for doing one good deed leads to doing yet another, and doing one transgression leads to doing yet another.

*Pirkei Avot 4:2*

# For Renewal, a Psalm

Happy is the person whom You discipline, Adonai,

The person You instruct in Your teaching,

To give him tranquillity in times of misfortune

Until a pit be dug for the wicked.

Adonai will not forsake the people.

You will not abandon your very own.

*Psalm 94:12-14*

# A Prayer

Our God and God of our ancestors, we acknowledge Your Torah as your guide. You gave a Law of righteousness to our ancestors. Your instructions were a lamp to their path and a light to their feet. May we, too, hearken to You, and serve You with a pure and perfect heart.

*Adapted from the morning liturgy*

# Personal Thoughts and Commitments
## for
## Self-Renewal This Week

# Ki Tisa: A Second Chance

## *Exodus 30:11-34:35*

**Resh Lakish said, "There are times when the abrogation of the Torah becomes the foundation of the Torah."**

*Babylonian Talmud, Menahot 99a-b*

- ✔ Now that the priests are consecrated, they are brought into service.
- ✔ In order to garner financial support for the priesthood, a census of the Israelite population is taken and a half-shekel assessment is made.
- ✔ Specific priestly accoutrements are described, including a special bowl which will help the priests maintain their own ritual purity.
- ✔ The priests are anointed.
- ✔ Bezalel and Oholiab are chosen to perform all of the tasks of building.
- ✔ Moses is late coming down from the mountain. And the people build the Golden Calf.
- ✔ In anger, Moses shatters the tablets and then goes back up the mountain.
- ✔ The covenant is renewed. Again, Moses goes up the mountain and remains there for forty days and forty nights.

## Sunday

**Moses said, "Oh, let me behold Your presence."**
*Exodus 33:18*

Sometimes, all we need is a little extra help. When we fail, we long for that second chance. Moses knew that failing feeling, and he yearned to see the presence of God, *kivyachol*—as if it were possible.

# *Monday*

**Adonai said to Moses: "I have seen this people, and
behold, it is a stiff-necked people."**
*Exodus 32:9*

Stiff-neckedness seems to be the Number One character
defect of the Jewish people. And the Book of Proverbs clearly
explains its danger: "He who stiffens his neck in stubbornness will suddenly be broken beyond repair" (29:1).

Someone set in his or her ways to the point of being broken
seems like a good working definition of an addict. What
could be more stubborn, or insane, than steadfastly refusing
to accommodate or even acknowledge that reality can
encroach on the limits of one's ego? Perhaps therein lies the
powerful appeal of drugs: They help to distort and jumble
reality to the point where even our own viewpoint is beside
the point. Getting high or being out of control from gambling
or sex made it easier for a while to dismiss any viewpoints or
feelings contrary to the ones we wanted to have.

But that time is far gone, even though we continued to use
long after the point of diminished returns. Stubbornness. A
feeling of futility. Active addiction is a pathetic mix of both.

Ironically, it is only after being "broken beyond repair" that
we can begin to admit the truth: That our stubborn denial of
our problem only aggravated the problem. As long as we
thought there was nothing wrong with us, nothing could be
made right.

Staying open and honest and developing closer relationships
with people who care about us enough to call us on our
scams will help ease the spiritual arthritis of stubbornness.
We need not waste any more time or energy defending the
indefensible.

# *Tuesday*

**The one who is truly wise foresees the
consequences of his own actions.**
*Babylonian Talmud, Tamid 32a*

"Moses saw that the people were out of control" (Exodus 32:25). Sometimes it takes someone else to show us the error of our ways. Sometimes it takes more than one person more than one time. But most of all, it is we who must recognize that our lives are out of control. It is we who must give ourselves a second chance and a third . . . if necessary. Believe in yourself. Then go out and become the best that you can be.

# *Wednesday*

**When God finished speaking with him on Mount Sinai,
God gave Moses the two tablets of the pact, stone tablets
inscribed with the finger of God.**
*Exodus 31:18*

What an image! Moses on the mountain, and God engraving the tablets. Now that you realize whom you're dealing with, when you get a second chance, take it.

# *Thursday*

## And when the people saw that Moses delayed to come down from the mount . . .
### *Exodus 32:1*

After returning from a spiritual weekend for recovering Jews, I, too, feel as if I am "coming down" from the spiritual heights and heady fellowship of the past few days. I didn't really want it to end. I never want the good times to end, but, alas, I have a family, responsibilities, and a life to return to.

Mystical encounters and illuminating insights are fine and sublime, but our tradition has never encouraged meditating on mountaintops our whole life—or even in study halls. There comes a time when we have to go back to the community, to apply our experience to everyday life, and to appreciate that there will be other spiritual growth opportunities on other days.

The Jewish Sabbath begins with candles being lit, and ends, at Havdalah, with a candle being extinguished. Where does the light go during the week? Ideally, it remains burning within us—in the hope that soon we will be temporarily redeemed by another Sabbath, in the renewed faith and strength that our day of rest has provided. This invisible, spiritual light can, for six days at least, guide us through the darkness of the mundane.

# *Friday*

## Write down these instructions, for in accordance with these instructions I make a covenant with you and with Israel.
### *Exodus 34:27*

God wants to make sure that Moses fully understands the requirements of the covenant—the rabbis say it is written with white fire on black fire. If you don't write things down, how will you ever remember them? When you write them down, read them aloud so that you can remember them.

# Shabbat

**You must keep my Sabbath for this is a sign between
Me and you throughout the ages, that you may know
that I Adonai have consecrated you. You shall keep
the Sabbath for it is holy for you.**

*Exodus 31:13-14*

Those in recovery have a special appreciation for the spiritual
value of stopping . . . and letting go. In the Serenity Prayer,
we acknowledge that God helps us to know what we can
change. On Shabbat we don't even ask the question. We simply demonstrate our belief in God as the One responsible for
all change. That's why our Sages tell us that whoever recites
Shabbat kiddush on Friday evening (which includes the biblical account of God's conclusion of creation) is considered to
be a partner in creation and thereby entitled to rest.

Shabbat is a second chance you get every week. Take advantage of it. Even when we lose our place in the world, Shabbat
is here to help us find it. What is it about Shabbat that gives
us that special sense of quietude, that affirms for us the
knowledge that God gives us opportunities time after time to
return? It is more than just rest. It is a total letting go. It is a
regeneration of the soul, a rebirth. On Shabbat, we do not
concern ourselves so much with what was as with what
might be. God offers us a glimpse of the future, what the
world might be, what we might look like—if only we would
work toward that goal. Like the Twelve Steps, we have to
work toward that goal all the time and keep working at it,
inching our way toward change. Shabbat and recovery: Both
are full of potential and the unlimited power to change our
world. And it comes every week just to remind you.

# Questions for Self-Reflection

1. What have I done to consecrate my life in service to God?

2. Where are the Golden Calves in my life, and how can I destroy them?

3. How can I improve my life to merit a second chance?

## Notes to Myself

# Sacred Thoughts for Holy Living

God said, "I hereby make a covenant. Before all your people I will make such wonders as have not been wrought in all the earth or in my nation. And all the people who are with you shall see how awesome are Adonai's deeds which I will perform for you."

*Exodus 34:10*

# For Renewal, A Psalm

Where can I flee from You?
If I rise high up to heaven,
You are there.
If I descend to hell,
You are there, too.
You know all my tricks and understand me better
    than I understand myself.
Search me, All-Knowing One
And know my thoughts.
Reveal my heart to all
And lead me from darkness to a better place.

*Adapted from Psalm 139*

# A Prayer

When we are weak, sustain us;
When we despair, open our hearts to joy.
When we are torn, lead us;
When we are tormented, touch us with tranquillity.
When we deceive, turn us to You;
When we corrupt, capture our hearts anew.
When we blunder, restore us.
With compassion, teach us that peace is based on Your truth.
And give us a second chance!

*Based on* Siddur Sim Shalom, *by Rabbi Jules Harlow*

# Personal Thoughts and Commitments
## for
## Self-Renewal This Week

# Vayakhel: Building Tabernacles

## Exodus 35:1-38:20

**Every assembly that is for the sake of Heaven
must in the end abide.**

*Pirkei Avot 4:11*

✔ Following the incident with the Golden Calf, Moses regains God's favor on behalf of Israel.

✔ Bezalel, the master craftsman, follows the "blueprint" and begins to build the Sanctuary.

✔ The Sabbath is introduced as a bridge which connects the building of the Tabernacle with its real purpose: to bring God and the people closer together.

## Sunday

**Thus, the Israelites, all the men and women whose
hearts moved them to bring anything for the work
that Adonai, through Moses, had commanded to be
done, brought a freewill offering to Adonai.**

*Exodus 35:29*

One by one, the Israelites brought their gifts to God. But it is not the gift God seeks, it is the giver.

# Monday

**And Moses assembled all the congregation and said:
"These are the words which Adonai has instructed that you
should do them. Six days shall work be done, but on the
seventh day there shall be to you a holy day . . .**
*Exodus 35:1-2*

Isn't "instructed that you should do them" a bit redundant?
Why else would God issue commands? But Jewish tradition
suggests that there is not one superfluous word in the Torah,
so there must be some explanation. And I think the language
here emphasizes the two-part nature of any communication:
the giving and the receiving, the talking and the listening, the
commanding and the doing.

Instructions—or even suggestions—are not complete until
they are actually done. The children of Israel say, "We will do
and we will hear"—which sounds great—but then they go
ahead and build a golden idol. God does not "talk to talk."
In a similar vein, talking about or even understanding the
Twelve Steps is not the same as doing them.

And what is the very first commandment that Moses conveys
to the assembled congregation of the children of Israel following the Golden Calf incident? To observe the Sabbath. To
give yourself a break. To disconnect—emotionally, physically,
and spiritually—from the trials and tribulations of the past
week. Only then, with restored perspective, are the Israelites
commanded to build something for God in place of the thing
that they had built as a god.

Time and time again in recovery, the past keeps interfering
with our present—and situations keep intruding on our serenity. Inner peace is often elusive, but *Shabbat shalom*—the peace
of Shabbat—is not. Learning to "do Shabbat right" is the traditional Jewish pathway to letting go. It has, most of the time,
worked for me. And it is never more than a week away.

# Tuesday

**If a person says to you, "I have worked and have not achieved," do not believe him. If a person says, "I have not worked, but still I have achieved," do not believe him. But if a person says, "I have worked, and I have achieved," you may believe him.**
*Babylonian Talmud, Megillah 6a*

Whether it is building a Tabernacle or working toward recovery, the results are the same. Work, and you will achieve. Don't work, and you aren't going anywhere.

# Wednesday

**The one who is humble brings God's presence close to earth to dwell among us.**
*Mechilta, Yitro*

If we are arrogant, there is no room for God, or for others, and certainly no room for recovery. If we are humble and accept the fact that we are not in control—that, in fact, our world has been out of control—then we can build a tabernacle, a place in our midst for God to dwell.

# *Thursday*

**And let every wise-hearted person among you come
and make all that Adonai has commanded.**

*Exodus 35:10*

I love the term "wise-hearted"—maybe because I have finally come to understand it. It says to me that there is a type of understanding that has nothing to do with one's intellect or education, a kind of emotional wisdom that is, perhaps, even more important to our mental and spiritual health. Any recovering person who never lost an argument but still felt like a loser will know exactly what I mean!

Very often, in my life, my intellectual understanding has surpassed my emotional comprehension of a situation. Or my willingness to try. But too much analyzing can be paralyzing. A recovering Jew might not have had the Jewish background to recognize the word *teshuvah* (repentance) and still be working a wonderful program. Conversely, a learned and observant Jew may know all the laws and still repeatedly relapse. This is the difference between heart-wisdom and head-wisdom. I had to learn it the hard way.

Probably the second-most popular Twelve Step slogan (right after "Easy does it") is "Keep it simple." But life so often refuses to cooperate! That's where heart-wisdom is necessary. In this week's portion, for instance, there is a detailed litany of instructions for building the tabernacle. They are anything but simple. And, yet, the basic principle linking all the "fine print" is quite simple: This is the way God wants it done. For the wise-hearted, that is enough.

# *Friday*

**The people are bringing more than is needed for
the tasks entailed in the work that Adonai has
commanded to be done.**

*Exodus 36:5*

That's our nature. If a little is good, more is even better. Enough already. Change the pattern. Stop the subterfuge. No more camouflage with alcohol, drugs, sex, food, or gambling. Let the real you shine forth. That tabernacle of self will stand.

# Shabbat

### . . . so the people stopped bringing.
### Exodus 36:6

You got the message. All we want is you; all God wants is you. Shabbat, in particular, is the time you can just be, not do. Stop trying to make up for things by giving gifts to the people you love and have hurt. The gifts, like your substance of choice, is illusory. It may make you think things are better, but only for a moment. Then you must return to face your life, which is as full or as empty as you have made it. Your family does not want your gifts. If you continue drinking and drugging, you won't be alive to enjoy them, anyway.

As we make progress in our recovery, we see more clearly the events of the past and the pain that accompanied it. Trying to rebuild what our addiction has destroyed is an awesome task. It might even be impossible. Not everything that is lost can be replaced. But we must realize that even as the memories become more distant and the pain recedes, they may never go away entirely. Nor should they. We are the product of our memories. It is the memory of our past which helps us to mold the future. More than anyone else, we as Jews understand the power and purpose of memory. Our collective memory reminds us of where we came from and where we are going. It defines us as individuals and as a people.

In recovery, we turn pain into gain. Listening to the newcomer's anguish "keeps us green." Recalling our own misery serves as an inspiring reminder to ourselves and to others that we don't have to live that way anymore . . . and that we have come a long way to get here.

If the pain of addiction was sufficient to get us into recovery, then it was pain with a purpose. We did not suffer for naught.

# Questions for Self-Reflection

1. What can I do to regain favor with God?

2. How shall I change my life so that it might be a Tabernacle for God?

3. What changes do I need to make to make my Shabbat truly a Sabbath of my soul?

## Notes to Myself

# Sacred Thoughts for Holy Living

We must not forget that it is not a thing that lends significance to a moment, it is a moment that lends significance to things.

*Abraham Joshua Heschel*

# For Renewal, A Psalm

One thing I request of Adonai
Only one thing shall I seek;
That I may dwell in the House of Adonai
All the days of my life,
To behold the pleasantness of Adonai
And to meditate in Your sanctum.

*Psalm 27:4*

# A Prayer

Close my eyes from evil and my ears from gossip, my heart from reflecting on unchaste thoughts and my mind from thinking of transgression. Guide my feet to walk in Your *mitzvot* and Your righteous path. May Your mercy be turned on me to be among those spared and preserved for life in Jerusalem.

*Babylonian Talmud, Berachot 17a*

# Personal Thoughts and Commitments
## for
## Self-Renewal This Week

# Pekudei: Nuts and Bolts

## Exodus 38:21-40:38

## Just as Adonai had instructed Moses, so the Israelites had done all the work.

*Exodus 39:42*

✔ Statistics. A summary of all the building materials used in the erection of the Tabernacle.

✔ In order to emphasize the importance and sanctity of the priesthood, the production of the priestly garden is again deserted.

✔ The priests and part of the Sanctuary are anointed.

✔ God tells Israel once again that the people are forgiven and the Divine presence is manifest in the midst of a cloud.

## Sunday

### He took the pact and put it in the Ark.

*Exodus 40:20*

While the search for the ancient Ark goes on, adventurers may be looking in the wrong place. The tablets represented the covenant, the Divine agreement, and the Israelites wanted to safeguard it. They put the tablets in the Ark and carried it high on their shoulders. But they placed the covenant in their hearts and sealed it with their deeds.

# Monday

## These are the accounts of the Tabernacle . . .
### *Exodus 38:21*

Why does the Torah go into so much detail about the construction and bill of materials for the Tabernacle and priestly vestments? Perhaps it is because we need it. On certain matters we can follow our hearts, but all the soul-searching in the world can't help us build a house. The only way to build a Tabernacle God's way is to listen to Divine instruction. Otherwise, we would just be doing it our way, which, as we know too well, sometimes puts us right back in Egypt.

If the Tabernacle and sacrificial rites are viewed as metaphors for prayer and opening up our hearts (as is the rabbinic consensus), three lessons may be drawn. One is that prayer is a two-way street: We must not forget to listen. The primary goal of prayer is not to present God with a shopping list of our needs, but to clear enough space within us to hearken to what God wants from us.

The second lesson is that the Tabernacle and vestments came into being from the collective effort of the people. Judaism has always valued group prayer over individual prayer. On Yom Kippur, we ask forgiveness as a people. Recovery, too, is a "we" program. It only works if we work it.

Finally, just as it is apparently important for us to learn the nuts-and-bolts makeup of the Tabernacle, so is it necessary for us to understand our own interior landscape. For this, an accounting of ourselves is helpful. It is called the Fourth Step: "Made a searching and fearless inventory of ourselves."

# Tuesday

**If one wants to be unclean, a person is given the opportunity. If one wants to be clean, that person is given Divine support.**
*Babylonian Talmud, Yoma 38b*

This is the nuts and bolts of recovery. You want it? It's yours. What else could you ask for?

# Wednesday

**Behold, I have refined you, but not with silver. I have chosen you in the furnace of affliction.**
*Isaiah 48:10*

Precious metals alone were insufficient to build the Tabernacle. It took the blood and sweat of men and women. That's what makes the metals precious.

# *Thursday*

### . . . a hundred sockets for the hundred talents, a talent for a socket.

*Exodus 38:7*

The *Shulchan Aruch,* the traditional code of Jewish law, states that "everyone is required to recite at least one hundred blessings a day" (Orach Chaim 46:3). That this number was identical to the number of sockets required for the Tabernacle was no coincidence, the Gerer Rebbe believed. Just as the sockets served as the foundation of the Sanctuary, he explained, so the daily blessings represent an individual's foundation of holiness.

Imagine thanking God one hundred times each day! Gratitude is one of the most spiritually powerful feelings we can have. It shifts our focus from feeling deprived or embittered by all the things we don't have to feeling appreciative for the many things we do.

Gratitude does not come naturally to most of us. We usually have no trouble finding something to complain about. But there is never any shortage of things to be grateful for in our lives; we just don't always see it that way.

To reach the level of spiritual depth where we can utter one hundred blessings each day may seem an unattainable goal. But it all begins by being grateful. Today, let us find at least one good thing to be grateful for . . . like our recovery. And let us say a prayer of thanks.

# *Friday*

### And when Moses saw that they had performed all the tasks—as Adonai had instructed, so they had done—Moses blessed them.

*Exodus 38:43*

When you finish the program, you get a special blessing: You get to continue. It doesn't sound like much at first, but it means you have survived. If you follow the program—as the Israelites did in building the Tabernacle—you will stay alive, and you will be able to bless others.

# *Shabbat*

**When Moses had finished all the work, the cloud covered the Tent of Meeting and the presence of Adonai filled the Tabernacle.**

*Exodus 40:33-34*

Now that's intense. The cloud enveloped the Israelites like a favorite garment protecting the wearer against the raw winter chill. Sometimes I think that it's the same cloud that wraps us up at Twelve Step meetings. You know the feeling. As soon as we enter the room, we feel different and protected, so much so that we linger afterwards. We really don't want to leave. But we have to do so. It's all part of recovery. Go to meetings and keep coming back.

When God placed the cloud over the Tent of Meeting, the Israelites felt God's presence but could see nothing else. It was not until the cloud was removed that the Israelites could continue their journey. The seasons of life have many moods. There is a time for silence and a time for grief; a time to embrace and a time to refrain from embracing. That is "life on life's terms." That's why you are in recovery: to learn how to accept those terms. By sharing life's triumphs and trials with friends in a fellowship community or in a synagogue, we can multiply our joys and divide our sorrows. One sage put it this way: Even the purest light causes shadows. There will be cloudy days, dark and gloomy. That's all part of recovery. But remember, there's light beyond the shadow.

# Questions for Self-Reflection

1. What "lists" do I still have to make?

2. How shall I convince myself of the sanctity of my life?

3. What do I have to go about doing in order to rebuild my life?

# Notes to Myself

# Sacred Thoughts for Holy Living

Regard as important the smallest victory that you win over the impulse to do evil. It may be to you a step to an even greater victory.

*Bachya ibn Pakuda,*
Duties of the Heart

# For Renewal, A Psalm

Unless Adonai builds the house,

Its builders labor in vain.

Unless Adonai watches over the city,

The guards keep vigil for nothing.

*Psalm 127:1*

# A Prayer

According to Maimonides in his *Mishneh Torah,* Hilchot Teshuvah (Perek 1), if a person commits a sin, he must confess his sins by saying the following: "I implore You, God. I sinned. I transgressed. I committed iniquity before You by doing _____. I have been chastened and shamed by what I have done. And for as long as I live, I shall not return to this act."

*This is the essential element (the nuts and bolts)*
*of the confessional prayer, says Maimonides.*

# Afterword

"Whoever saves a single soul, it is as if that person saves an entire universe" (Babylonian Talmud, Sanhedrin 19b). There are few things as soul-destroying as living with a chemical dependency or an addiction to a compulsive behavior. The many thousands of Jews in recovery can, like Aaron Z., testify to the emotional, spiritual, and physical bankruptcy the disease forces on individuals and families.

This does not have to be the case. Recovery is possible and life can not only go on, but it can be celebrated with warmth and wisdom, richness and meaning. That's the message of this book. Indeed that's the message JACS sends out on a daily basis to the Jewish community across North America and beyond

JACS was formed thirteen years ago by a small gathering of Jews to explore the wisdom and richness of the Jewish tradition in relation to their own recovery. It has now grown to an organization that affects the lives of thousands through an active membership organization, retreats, conferences, lecture series, newsletters, chavurot, and professional training and outreach to the Jewish community.

JACS is grateful to Rabbi Kerry Olitzky for carrying the message about addiction and recovery on a national level. In his first book on recovery and renewal, *Twelve Jewish Steps to Recovery,* Rabbi Olitzky (and Dr. Stuart Copans) put to rest the misconception that the Twelve Step recovery process is not compatible with Jewish tradition and belief. While the book was intended to help those in the Twelve Step programs articulate the bond of Judaism and recovery, it also had a secondary effect: To help dent the wall of denial about substance abuse that still exists in the Jewish community. This work is invaluable. The myth that Jews are not addicts is not only untrue, but it also prevents many from the opportunity for *teshuvah,* return that is implicit in the Jewish heritage.

How do you breach that wall of denial for yourself, for your family or community? Reading *Renewed Each Day* is the first step. Going to Alcoholics Anonymous, Alanon, and other applicable Twelve Step programs is the second and most crucial step for everyone, including members of the Jewish community.

JACS helps people find the resources within our community and tradition to recover and move forward with their lives. The first of these resources is available to all, regardless of religious orientation, through AA and other Twelve Step programs. We know from a personal basis that AA works, that the foundations of the Twelve Step programs are consistent with the teachings of Judaism. Once you have laid the foundation for your recovery, you can begin to reaccess the wealth of spiritual resources in Jewish tradition through its literature, practice, programs, and community.

JACS, again, is grateful to Rabbi Olitzky, and to Aaron Z., for this second book, which provides tools for that process of spiritual renewal through daily meditations. These selections of sacred text present a wonderful opportunity to enhance the recovery process from the perspective of Jewish tradition and belief, as JACS does through its many contacts and activities, providing help to access our age-old Jewish legacy of healing, compassion, and care to those in the Jewish community concerned with addiction and recovery.

TAMI CRYSTAL, Executive Director
DAVID BUCHHOLZ, President
The JACS Foundation,
New York City

## About Jewish Lights

People of all faiths and backgrounds yearn for books that attract, engage, educate, and spiritually inspire.

Our principal goal is to stimulate thought and help all people learn about who the Jewish People are, where they come from, and what the future can be made to hold. While people of our diverse Jewish heritage are the primary audience, our books speak to people in the Christian world as well and will broaden their understanding of Judaism and the roots of their own faith.

We bring to you authors who are at the forefront of spiritual thought and experience. While each has something different to say, they all say it in a voice that you can hear.

Our books are designed to welcome you and then to engage, stimulate, and inspire. We judge our success not only by whether or not our books are beautiful and commercially successful, but by whether or not they make a difference in your life.

For your information and convenience, at the back of this book we have provided a list of other Jewish Lights books you might find interesting and useful. They cover all the categories of your life:

| | |
|---|---|
| Bar/Bat Mitzvah | Life Cycle |
| Bible Study / Midrash | Meditation |
| Children's Books | Men's Interest |
| Congregation Resources | Parenting |
| Current Events / History | Prayer / Ritual / Sacred Practice |
| Ecology / Environment | Social Justice |
| Fiction: Mystery, Science Fiction | Spirituality |
| Grief / Healing | Theology / Philosophy |
| Holidays / Holy Days | Travel |
| Inspiration | Twelve Steps |
| Kabbalah / Mysticism / Enneagram | Women's Interest |

**For more information about each book, visit our website at www.jewishlights.com**

# About the Contributors

**RABBI KERRY M. OLITZKY, D.H.L.,** is executive director of the Jewish Outreach Institute. He has been a trendsetter in developing training programs for clergy and other professionals, especially in the area of addiction and chemical dependency. Rabbi Olitzky is the author or co-author of many books on Jewish spirituality, healing and Jewish religious practice, including *100 Blessings Every Day: Daily Twelve Step Recovery Affirmations, Exercises for Personal Growth & Renewal Reflecting Seasons of the Jewish Year; Renewed Each Day, Vol. 1 & Vol. 2: Daily Twelve Step Recovery Meditations Based on the Bible;* and *Twelve Jewish Steps to Recovery: A Personal Guide to Turning from Alcoholism and Other Addictions* (all Jewish Lights).

**AARON Z.** is a recovering person who shares his personal insights and experiences with others who seek help. He is active in his synagogue and chairperson of his area's JACS group (Jewish Alcoholics, Chemically Dependent Persons and Significant Others Foundation).

**TAMI CRYSTAL AND DAVID BUCHHOLZ** were executive director and president, respectively, of The JACS Foundation (Jewish Alcoholics, Chemically Dependent Persons and Significant Others) in New York City.

**RABBI HAROLD M. SCHULWEIS** of Temple Valley Beth Shalom in Encino, California, is widely recognized as an innovative and inspiring religious educator. His work has been especially sensitive to the dilemmas and struggles of contemporary life.

# About the Art

The cover art and ornamentation of this book are from artist MATY GRÜNBERG's striking portfolio of the twelve gates of the Old City of Jurusalem. This art emphasizes the relationship between heavenly and earthly in all our lives through the prism of Jerusalem.

Grünberg is an Israeli artist who has made his home in London since the late 1960s. His illuminated books and sculptures are found in the collections of museums and institutions throughout the world.

*Beautiful prints of this inspiring art are available for purchase from Jewish Lights Publishing.*